Jerom

After

Ghost
Stories

Jerome Klapka Jerome (1859 - 1927) was born in Walsall, England. He is famous for his elegant humour and lively comedy. His most famous books *("Three men on a boat", "Three men on the Bummel")*, written in the last decade of the nineteenth century, combine lively observation of the social ironies of Victorian England with a comic and sentimental vein which make them irresistible to a wide audience. He achieved great popularity with these books, which were translated into many languages. He also produced some brilliant journalism, in particular between 1892 and 1897. He died in Northampton, England.

La Spiga
LANGUAGES

INTRODUCTORY

Twas Christmas Eve.

I begin this way, because it is the proper, orthodox, respectable way to begin, and I have been brought up in a proper, orthodox, respectable way, and taught to always do the proper, orthodox, respectable thing; and the habit clings to me.

Of course, as a mere matter of information it is quite unnecessary to mention the date at all. The experienced reader knows it was Christmas Eve, without my telling him. It always is Christmas Eve, in a ghost story.

Christmas Eve is the ghosts' great gala night. On Christmas Eve they hold their annual fête. On Christmas Eve everybody in Ghostland who *is* anybody - or rather, speaking of ghosts, one should say, I suppose, every nobody who *is* any nobody - comes out to show himself or herself, to see and to be seen, to promenade about and display their winding-sheets and grave-clothes to each other, to criticize one another's style, and sneer at one another's complexion.

"Christmas Eve parade", as I expect they themselves term it, is a function, doubtless, eagerly prepared for and looked forward to throughout Ghostland, especially by the swagger set, such as the murdered Barons, the crime-stained Countesses, and the Earls who came over with the Conqueror, and assassinated their relatives, and died raving mad. Hollow moans and fiendish grins are, one may be sure, energetically practised up. Blood-curdling shrieks and marrow-freezing gestures are probably rehearsed for weeks beforehand. Rusty chains and gory daggers are overhauled, and put into good working order; and sheets and shrouds, laid carefully by from the previous year's show, are taken down and shaken out, and mended, and aired.

Oh, it is a stirring night in Ghostland, the night of December the twenty-fourth!

Ghosts never come out on Christmas night itself, you may have noticed. Christmas Eve, we suspect, has been too much for them; they are not used to excitement. For about a week after Christmas Eve, the gentlemen ghosts, no doubt, feel as if they were all head, and go about making solemn resolutions to themselves that they will stop in next

Twas: it was. **Christmas Eve**: the day before Christmas, 24th December.
brought up: educated, raised.

clings to: remains with.

mere: pure, simple. **quite**: completely.
mention: speak about.

gala: celebration.
fête: party, festival.
everybody who *is* anybody: all the important members.
nobody who *is* any nobody: play on words: a ghost is nobody.
promenade: walk.
display: show. **winding-sheets**: coverings for dead body.
grave: tomb. **sneer**: make rude comments about.
complexion: skin.
term: call.
function: party, social occasion. **eagerly**: keenly, with enthusiasm. **looked forward to**: waited for. **throughout**: in all of.
swagger set: the elite, the most snobbish. **stained**: with the marks of. **the Conqueror**: William the Conqueror, Norman King who successfully invaded England in 1066. **came over with the Conqueror**: the oldest aristocracy. **raving mad**: completely crazy, screaming and shouting. **Hollow**: with a frightening sound.
fiendish: diabolical. **grins**: strange smiles. **Blood-curdling**: makes the blood thick from fear. **shrieks**: screams, shouts.
marrow: bone-marrow, the substance inside bones. **rehearsed**: practised before a performance. **beforehand**: before, previously.
Rusty: oxidised. **gory**: covered with blood. **daggers**: short knives.
overhauled: repaired. **shrouds**: coverings worn in the tomb.
shaken out: the dust is removed. **aired**: exposed to the air. **stirring**: exciting.

solemn: serious. **stop in**: stay at home.

Christmas Eve; while the lady spectres are contradictory and snappish, and liable to burst into tears and leave the room hurriedly on being spoken to, for no perceptible cause whatever.

Ghosts with no position to maintain - mere middle-class ghosts - occasionally, I believe, do a little haunting on off-nights: on All-hallows Eve, and at Midsummer; and some will even run up for a mere local event - to celebrate, for instance, the anniversary of the hanging of somebody's grandfather, or to prophesy a misfortune.

He does love prophesying a misfortune, does the average British ghost. Send him out to prognosticate trouble to somebody, and he is happy. Let him force his way into a peaceful home, and turn the whole house upside down by foretelling a funeral, or predicting a bankruptcy, or hinting at a coming disgrace, or some other terrible disaster, about which nobody in their senses would want to know sooner than they could possibly help, and the prior knowledge of which can serve no useful purpose whatsoever, and he feels that he is combining duty with pleasure. He would never forgive himself if anybody in his family had a trouble and he had not been there for a couple of months beforehand, doing silly tricks on the lawn, or balancing himself on somebody's bed-rail.

Then there are, besides, the very young, or very conscientious ghosts with a lost will or an undiscovered number weighing heavy on their minds, who will haunt steadily all the year round; and also the fussy ghost, who is indignant at having been buried in the dust-bin or in the village pond, and who never gives the parish a single night's quiet until somebody has paid for a first-class funeral for him.

But these are the exceptions. As I have said, the average orthodox ghost does his one turn a year, on Christmas Eve, and is satisfied.

Why on Christmas Eve, of all nights in the year, I never could myself understand. It is invariably one of the most dismal nights to be out in - cold, muddy, and wet. And besides, at Christmas time, everybody has quite enough to put up with in the way of a houseful of living relations, without wanting the ghosts of any dead ones mooning about the place, I am sure.

There must be something ghostly in the air of Christmas -

4

spectres: ghosts.
snappish: irritable, bad-tempered. **liable to**: with a tendency to.
hurriedly: very quickly. **perceptible**: which can be perceived or imagined.
position: social position. **mere**: simple, only.
haunting: the appearance of ghosts in a house or other place.
off-nights: nights which are not so busy. **All-hallows Eve**: *31st October*. **Midsummer**: *24th June*. **run up**: appear.
hanging: execution with a rope.
prophesy: predict. **misfortune**: bad luck.

prognosticate: predict.

turn... upside down: create confusion.
foretelling: predicting. **bankruptcy**: state of being bankrupt, financial failure of a business. **hinting**: making suggestions about.
disgrace: disaster. **nobody in their senses**: nobody who is not mad. **sooner**: earlier. **prior**: previous. **knowledge**: knowing.
purpose: aim, goal. **whatsoever**: at all.
duty: moral obligation.
trouble: problem.
couple of: about two. **beforehand**: earlier.
silly: stupid, childish. **tricks**: illusions, entertainment. **lawn**: grass. **bed-rail**: the tube at the foot of a bed.
besides: in addition, as well, also.
conscientious: with a strong moral sense. **will**: testament.
undiscovered: not found. **weighing heavy on their minds**: preoccupying them a lot. **who will haunt steadily**: who habitually make their appearance at regular intervals. *Note the use of will to indicate habit.* **fussy**: fastidious, obsessed with small details.
indignant: very angry. **buried**: put under the ground when dead.
dust-bin: container for rubbish. **village pond**: small lake in village.
parish: administrative district of the Church.
exceptions: unusual cases.

invariably: always.
dismal: depressing. **muddy**: dirty.

put up with: tolerate.
mooning: looking miserable.

something about the close, muggy atmosphere that draws up the ghosts, like the dampness of the summer rains brings out the frogs and snails.

And not only do the ghosts themselves always walk on Christmas Eve, but live people always sit and talk about them on Christmas Eve. Whenever five or six English-speaking people meet round a fire on Christmas Eve, they start telling each other ghost stories. Nothing satisfies us on Christmas Eve but to hear each other tell authentic anecdotes about spectres. It is a genial, festive season, and we love to muse upon graves, and dead bodies, and murders, and blood.

There is a good deal of similarity about our ghostly experiences; but this of course is not our fault but the fault of the ghosts, who never will try any new performances, but always will keep steadily to the old, safe business. The consequence is that, when you have been at one Christmas Eve party, and heard six people relate their adventures with spirits, you do not require to hear any more ghost stories. To listen to any further ghost stories after that would be like sitting out farcical comedies, or taking in two comic journals; the repetition would become wearisome.

There is always the young man who was, one year, spending the Christmas at a country house, and, on Christmas Eve, they put him to sleep in the west wing. Then in the middle of the night, the room door quietly opens and somebody - generally a lady in her night-dress - walks slowly in, and comes and sits on the bed. The young man thinks it must be one of the visitors, or some relative of the family, though he does not remember having previously seen her, who, unable to go to sleep, and feeling lonesome, all by herself, has come into his room for a chat. He has no idea it is a ghost: he is so unsuspicious. She does not speak, however; and, when he looks again, she is gone!

The young man relates the circumstance at the breakfast-table next morning, and asks each of the ladies present if it were she who was his visitor. But they all assure him that it was not, and the host, who has grown deadly pale, begs him to say no more about the matter, which strikes the young man as a singularly strange request.

After breakfast the host takes the young man into a corner, and explains to him that what he saw was the ghost of a lady

close, muggy: humid, suffocating.
draws up: attracts. **dampness**: wet.
frogs: small green amphibians. **snails**: molluscs carrying their shells on their backs.
live: alive, still living.

Nothing satisfies us… but: the only thing which satisfies us is…
authentic: real. **anecdotes**: stories. **spectres**: ghosts. **genial**: happy. **festive**: celebratory. **season**: time of year. **muse**: meditate. **graves**: tombs.
a good deal of: a lot of.
fault: negative characteristic.

steadily: regularly.

relate: tell.
require: need.
any further: any more.
sitting out: sitting and watching a complete play. **taking in**: subscribing to. **wearisome**: tiring, boring.

west wing: the western area of a big house.

though: even if. **previously**: before.
unable: incapable. **lonesome**: lonely.
chat: informal talk.
unsuspicious: not suspecting anything.

relates: tells. **circumstance**: event, happening.

if it were she: note use of subject pronoun after verb to be: this is rare in modern English. **assure**: tell him with certainty. **host**: person giving hospitality. **deadly pale**: as white as a dead person. **begs**: asks with insistence. **strikes**: seems to. **singularly**: very, unusually.

who had been murdered in that very bed, or who had murdered somebody else there - it does not really matter which: you can be a ghost by murdering somebody else or by being murdered yourself, whichever you prefer. The murdered ghost is, perhaps, the more popular; but, on the other hand, you can frighten people better if you are the murdered one, because then you can show your wounds and do groans.

Then there is the sceptical guest - it is always "the guest" who gets let in for this sort of thing, by-the-bye. A ghost never thinks much of his own family: it is "the guest" he likes to haunt who after listening to the host's ghost story, on Christmas Eve, laughs at it, and says that he does not believe there are such things as ghosts at all; and that he will sleep in the haunted chamber that very night, if they will let him.

Everybody urges him not to be reckless, but he persists in his foolhardiness, and goes up to the Yellow Chamber (or whatever colour the haunted room may be) with a light heart and a candle, and wishes them all good-night, and shuts the door.

Next morning he has got snow-white hair.

He does not tell anybody what he has seen: it is too awful.

There is also the plucky guest, who sees a ghost, and knows it is a ghost, and watches it, as it comes into the room and disappears through the wainscot, after which, as the ghost does not seem to be coming back, and there is nothing, consequently, to be gained by stopping awake, he goes to sleep.

He does not mention having seen the ghost to anybody, for fear of frightening them - some people are so nervous about ghosts - but determines to wait for the next night, and see if the apparition appears again.

It does appear again, and, this time, he gets out of bed, dresses himself and does his hair, and follows it; and then discovers a secret passage leading from the bedroom down into the beer-cellar - a passage which, no doubt, was not unfrequently made use of in the bad old days of yore.

After him comes the young man who woke up with a strange sensation in the middle of the night, and found his rich bachelor uncle standing by his bedside. The rich uncle smiled a weird sort of smile and vanished. The young man

that very bed: precisely that bed.

frighten: scare.
wounds: injuries, cuts.
groans: cries of pain.
sceptical: someone who is not convinced easily. **guest**: person receiving hospitality. **gets let in for**: is exposed to. **by-the-bye**: by the way.
haunt: appear to.

chamber: room.

urges: persuades strongly. **reckless**: foolish, risky. **persists**: continues, insists. **foolhardiness**: risky behaviour.

snow-white: as white as snow.
awful: terrible.
plucky: courageous.

wainscot: wooden section at the bottom of a wall.

nothing … to be gained: no profit can be had.

mention: speak about.

determines: decides.
apparition: ghost.

discovers: finds.
beer-cellar: underground room where beer is kept at a cool temperature. **not unfrequently**: often. **of yore**: in the past.

bachelor: unmarried man.
weird: strange.

immediately got up and looked at his watch. It had stopped at half-past four, he having forgotten to wind it.

He made inquiries the next day, and found that, strangely enough, his rich uncle, whose only nephew he was, had married a widow with eleven children at exactly a quarter to twelve, only two days ago.

The young man does not attempt to explain the extraordinary circumstance. All he does is to vouch for the truth of his narrative. And, to mention another case, there is the gentleman who is returning home late at night, from a Freemasons' dinner, and who, noticing a light issuing from a ruined abbey, creeps up, and looks through the keyhole. He sees the ghost of a "grey sister" kissing the ghost of a brown monk, and is so inexpressibly shocked and frightened that he faints on the spot, and is discovered there the next morning, lying in a heap against the door, still speechless, and with his faithful latch-key clasped tightly in his hand.

All these things happen on Christmas Eve, they are all told of on Christmas Eve. For ghost stories to be told on any other evening than the evening of the twenty-fourth of December would be impossible in English society as at present regulated. Therefore, in introducing the sad but authentic ghost stories that follow hereafter, I feel that it is unnecessary to inform the student of Anglo-Saxon literature that the date on which they were told and on which the incidents took place was - Christmas Eve.

Nevertheless, I do so.

Comprehension Questions

1. How has the writer been taught to do things?
2. Why is it quite unnecessary for the writer to mention the fact that it is Christmas Eve?
3. Why is Christmas Eve important for ghosts? What do they do?
4. Which ghosts in particular look forward to Christmas Eve?
5. What do the ghosts do in preparation?
6. Why does the writer suspect ghosts never come out on Christmas night?
7. How do gentlemen and lady ghosts behave the week after Christmas? Why?
8. What kind of ghosts appear on other occasions?
9. What does the typical English ghost love doing?
10. Which ghosts haunt every night?
11. Why does the writer think Christmas Eve is a strange night for the ghosts to pick?
12. What is meant by "There must be something ghostly in the

wind: turn in order to put tension into a spring.

nephew: inverse relation to uncle *(son of a brother or sister)*.
widow: woman who has lost her husband.

circumstance: event, happening. **vouch for**: guarantee.
narrative: story.

Freemasons: secret society. **issuing**: coming out
ruined: falling down. **abbey**: religious building. **creeps up**:
approaches very quietly. **keyhole**: hole in door where key is
inserted. **sister**: nun, religious woman. **monk**: religious man.
inexpressibly: impossible to express. **faints**: loses consciousness. **on the spot**: there and then, immediately. **discovered**:
found. **heap**: pile. **speechless**: not able to talk. **faithful**: always
carried with him. **latch-key**: key to a door. **clasped**: held. **tightly**:
strongly.

Therefore: so.
authentic: realistic. **hereafter**: after this.

Nevertheless: in spite of this, but.

air of Christmas - something about the close, muggy atmosphere that draws up the ghosts, like the dampness of the
summer rains brings out the frogs and snails"?
13. What do live people invariably do on Christmas Eve?
14. Why do you think people love to "muse upon graves, and
dead bodies, and murders, and blood" at this time? Is this
true in your experience?
15. How does the writer explain the fact that ghost stories are all
more or less the same? Whose fault is this?
16. What examples does he give of typical ghost stories?
17. What is meant by "He has no idea it is a ghost: he is so
unsuspicious"?
18. Why is the murdered ghost the more popular?
19. What usually happens to the "sceptical guest" in the stories?
20. What does the "plucky guest" usually do?
21. Why do you think the rich uncle smiles "a weird sort of smile"
before vanishing?
22. What happens when the gentleman sees the ghost of a "grey
sister" kissing the ghost of a "brown monk"? Why?

HOW THE STORIES
CAME TO BE TOLD

It was Christmas Eve! Christmas Eve at my Uncle John's;
Christmas Eve (There is too much 'Christmas Eve' about
this book. I can see that myself. It is beginning to get
monotonous even to me. But I don't see how to avoid it
now.) at No. 47 Laburnham Grove, Tooting! Christmas
Eve in the dimly-lighted (there was a gas-strike on) front
parlour, where the flickering firelight threw strange shadows
on the highly coloured wall-paper, while without, in the
wild street, the storm raged pitilessly, and the wind, like some
unquiet spirit, flew, moaning, across the square, and passed,
wailing with a troubled cry, round by the milk-shop.
We had had supper, and were sitting round, talking and
smoking.
We had had a very good supper - a very good supper,
indeed. Unpleasantness has occurred since, in our family,
in connection with this party. Rumours have been put about
in our family, concerning the matter generally, but more
particularly concerning my own share in it, and remarks
have been passed which have not so much surprised me,
because I know what our family are, but which have pained
me very much. As for my Aunt Maria, I do not know when
I shall care to see her again. I should have thought Aunt
Maria might have known me better.
But although injustice - gross injustice, as I shall explain
later on - has been done to myself, that shall not deter me
from doing justice to others; even to those who have made
unfeeling insinuations. I will do justice to Aunt Maria's hot
veal pasties, and toasted lobsters, followed by her own
special make of cheesecakes, warm (there is no sense, to
my thinking, in cold cheesecakes; you lose half the flavour), and washed down by Uncle John's own particular
old ale, and acknowledge that they were most tasty. I did
justice to them then; Aunt Maria herself could not but
admit that.
After supper, Uncle brewed some whisky-punch. I did
justice to that also; Uncle John himself said so. He said he
was glad to notice that I liked it.
Aunt went to bed soon after supper, leaving the local

12

Tooting: suburb of London, south of the river Thames.
dimly-lighted: not well illuminated. **gas-strike**: no work was done by the men supplying gas for lamps. **front parlour**: front room.
flickering: constantly changing. **firelight**: light from an open fire.
without: outside. **raged**: made a terrible noise, like being angry.
pitilessly: without pity. **moaning**: making a crying noise. **wailing**: crying like a child. **troubled**: worried.

Unpleasantness: disagreement, nasty things.
Rumours: gossip, unjustified talk.

share: part.

pained: hurt.
care: want.

injustice: wrong, unfair action. **gross**: great.
deter: prevent.

unfeeling: cruel.
veal pasties: meat pies. **lobsters**: very prestigious shellfish.

flavour: taste.

ale: beer. **acknowledge**: recognize. **tasty**: good to eat.
I did justice to them: I ate a lot of them.
could not but admit: could only admit.
brewed: prepared a drink. **whisky-punch**: hot drink containing whisky.
glad: happy.

curate, old Dr Scrubbles, Mr Samuel Coombes, our member of the County Council, Teddy Biffles, and myself to keep Uncle company. We agreed that it was too early to give in for some time yet, so Uncle brewed another bowl of punch; and I think we all did justice to that - at least I know I did. It is a passion with me, is the desire to do justice.

We sat up for a long while, and the Doctor brewed some gin-punch later on, for a change, though I could not taste much difference myself. But it was all good, and we were very happy- everybody was so kind.

Uncle John told us a very funny story in the course of the evening. Oh, it *was* a funny story! I forget what it was about now, but I know it amused me very much at the time; I do not think I ever laughed so much in all my life. It is strange that I cannot recollect that story too, because he told it us four times. And it was entirely our own fault that he did not tell it us a fifth. After that, the Doctor sang a very clever song, in the course of which he imitated all the different animals in a farmyard. He did mix them a bit. He brayed for the bantam cock, and crowed for the pig; but we knew what he meant all right.

I started relating a most interesting anecdote, but was somewhat surprised to observe, as I went on, that nobody was paying the slightest attention to me whatever. I thought this rather rude of them at first, until it dawned upon me that I was talking to myself all the time, instead of out aloud, so that, of course, they did not know that I was telling them a tale at all, and were probably puzzled to understand the meaning of my animated expression and eloquent gestures. It was a most curious mistake for any one to make. I never knew such a thing happen to me before.

Later on, our curate did tricks with cards. He asked us if we had ever seen a game called the "Three Card Trick".

He said it was an artifice by means of which low, unscrupulous men, frequenters of race-meetings and suchlike haunts, swindled foolish young fellows out of their money. He said it was a very simple trick to do: it all depended on the quickness of the hand. It was the quickness of the hand deceived the eye.

He said he would show us the imposture so that we might be warned against it, and not be taken in by it; and he fetched Uncle's pack of cards from the tea-caddy, and,

curate: priest.
County Council: local administrative body.
to give in: to go to bed.
bowl: large receptacle for liquids.

desire: wish.
while: time.
though: even if.

amused me: made me laugh.

recollect: remember.
entirely: completely. **fault**: negative characteristic.

He brayed: he made a noise like a donkey.
bantam: type of cock. **(he) crowed**: (he) made a noise like a cock.
relating: telling. **anecdote**: story.
somewhat: quite. **went on**: continued.
paying the slightest attention: listening at all.
it dawned upon me: I realised suddenly.
out aloud: to other people.
tale: story. **puzzled**: perplexed.
animated expression: the lively look on my face.
eloquent: expressive.
curious: strange.

tricks with cards: illusions with cards.

artifice: illusion, art. **low**: socially inferior.
unscrupulous: without scruples. **frequenters of race-meetings**: people who often went to horse-races. **suchlike haunts**: similar places. **swindled**: tricked, deceived. **foolish**: stupid.
fellows: men.
deceived: tricked.
imposture: trick.
warned: told of a dangerous possibility. **taken in**: tricked.
fetched: got, procured. **tea-caddy**: container for tea.

selecting three cards from the pack, two plain cards and one picture card, sat down on the hearthrug, and explained to us what he was going to do.

He said: "Now I shall take these three cards in my hand - so - and let you all see them. And then I shall quietly lay them down on the rug, with the backs uppermost, and ask you to pick out the picture card. And you'll think you know which one it is." And he did it.

Old Mr Coombes, who is also one of our church-wardens, said it was the middle card.

"You fancy you saw it," said our curate, smiling.

"I don't 'fancy' anything at all about it," replied Mr Coombes. "I tell you it's the middle card. I'll bet you half a dollar it's the middle card."

"There you are, that's just what I was explaining to you," said our curate, turning to the rest of us; "that's the way these foolish young fellows that I was speaking of are lured on to lose their money. They make sure they know the card, they fancy they saw it. They don't grasp the idea that it is the quickness of the hand that has deceived their eye."

He said he had known young men go off to a boat race, or a cricket match, with pounds in their pocket, and come home, early in the afternoon, stone broke; having lost all their money at this demoralizing game.

He said he should take Mr Coombes's half-crown, because it would teach Mr Coombes a very useful lesson, and probably be the means of saving Mr Coombes's money in the future; and he should give the two-and-sixpence to the blanket fund.

"Don't you worry about that," retorted old Mr Coombes. "Don't you take the half-crown *out* of the blanket fund - that's all."

And he put his money on the middle card, and turned it up. Sure enough, it really was the queen!

We were all very much surprised, especially the curate.

He said that it did sometimes happen that way, though - that a man did sometimes lay on the right card, by accident.

Our curate said it was, however, the most unfortunate thing a man could do for himself, if he only knew it, because, when a man tried and won, it gave him a taste for the so-called sport, and it lured him on into risking again and again; until he had to retire from the contest, a broken and

plain cards: *cards with numbers only*.
picture cards: cards with pictures: *Jack, Queen, King*. **hearth-rug**: carpet in front of the fire.

uppermost: on top.
pick out: select.

church-wardens: church officials.

fancy: imagine, think.

bet: offer money to support an idea.
half a dollar: *(London slang) 2 shillings and sixpence*.

lured on: attracted.
grasp: understand.

cricket match: *summer sporting event in England*.
stone broke: without any money at all.
demoralizing: depressing.
half-crown: two shillings and sixpence.

means: method.

blanket fund: money collected by the Church to provide blankets for the poor.

though: however.
lay: bet. **by accident**: by chance.

taste: enthusiasm, passion.
so-called: presumed. **lured him on**: tempted him, attracted him.

ruined man.

Then he did the trick again. Mr Coombes said it was the card next the coal-scuttle this time, and wanted to put five shillings on it.

We laughed at him, and tried to persuade him against it. He would listen to no advice, however, but insisted on plunging.

Our curate said very well then: he had warned him, and that was all that he could do. If he (Mr Coombes) was determined to make a fool of himself, he (Mr Coombes) must do so.

Our curate said he should take the five shillings and that would put things right again with the blanket fund.

So Mr Coombes put two half-crowns on the card next the coal-scuttle and turned it up.

Sure enough, it was the queen again!

After that, Uncle John had a florin on, and *he* won.

And then we all played at it; and we all won. All except the curate, that is. He had a very bad quarter of an hour. I never knew a man have such hard luck at cards. He lost every time.

He had some more punch after that; and Uncle made such a funny mistake in brewing it: he left out the whisky. Oh, we did laugh at him, and we made him put in double quantity afterwards, as a forfeit.

Oh, we did have such fun that evening!

And then, somehow or other, we must have got on to ghosts; because the next recollection I have is that we were telling ghost stories to each other.

Comprehension Questions

1. Where is the writer on Christmas Eve?
2. What kind of evening is it?
3. Why is the parlour "dimly-lighted"?
4. What has happened in the family since that supper? Why?
5. What is meant by "remarks have been passed which have not so much surprised me, because I know what our family are, but which have pained me very much"?
6. What is meant by "that shall not deter me from doing justice to others" and "I did justice" to Aunt Maria's warm cheese-cakes? What is the difference between the two forms of "justice"?
7. What do they do after Aunt Maria goes to bed?
8. Why do you think the writer does not notice much difference

ruined: financially destroyed.

coal-scuttle: container for coal, a solid black fuel.

plunging: betting his money.
warned him: told him about the dangers.

make a fool of himself: appear very stupid in front of the others.

florin: two shillings. **had a florin on**: bet two shillings on a card.

hard luck: bad luck.

brewing: preparing a drink.
we did laugh: *Note the use of did to reinforce the idea of laughing.*
forfeit: punishment.
fun: a good time, enjoyment.
somehow or other: in some way. **got on to**: proceeded to.
recollection: memory.

---

    between the whisky-punch and the gin-punch?
9.   Why do you think he can't remember Uncle John's funny story?
10. How does the doctor amuse them?
11. Why is the writer's own story not appreciated by the others?
12. What is the "Three Card Trick"?
13. Why does the curate show them this trick? Who normally uses it? On what does the trick depend?
14. Why does the curate take Mr Coombes's half-crown?
15. What does the curate say he will do with the money he wins?
16. How does the curate explain Mr Coombes's first win?
17. What happens the second time?
18. Who is the only person who doesn't have luck that evening? What happens? Why ?
19. Why do they make Uncle John put a double quantity of whisky in the punch?

TEDDY BIFFLES' STORY

Teddy Biffles told the first story. I will let him repeat it here in his own words.

(Do not ask me how it is that I recollect his own exact words - whether I took them down in shorthand at the time, or whether he had the story written out, and handed me the MS afterwards for publication in this book, because I should not tell you if you did. It is a trade secret.)

Biffles called his story:-

JOHNSON AND EMILY
or
THE FAITHFUL GHOST
(Teddy Biffles' Story)

I was little more than a lad when I first met with Johnson. I was home for the Christmas holidays, and, it being Christmas Eve, I had been allowed to sit up very late. On opening the door of my little bedroom, to go in, I found myself face to face with Johnson, who was coming out. It passed through me, and uttering a long low wail of misery, disappeared out of the staircase window.

I was startled for the moment - I was only a schoolboy at the time, and had never seen a ghost before - and felt a little nervous about going to bed. But, on reflection, I remembered that it was only sinful people that spirits could do any harm to, and so tucked myself up, and went to sleep.

In the morning I told the Pater what I had seen.

"Oh yes, that was old Johnson," he answered. "Don't you be frightened of that; he lives here." And then he told me the poor thing's history.

It seemed that Johnson, when it was alive, had loved, in early life, the daughter of a former lessee of our house, a very beautiful girl, whose Christian name had been Emily. Father did not know her other name.

Johnson was too poor to marry the girl, so he kissed her good-bye, told her he would soon be back, and went off to Australia to make his fortune.

But Australia was not then what it became later on. Travellers through the bush were few and far between in

took them down in shorthand: wrote them in a special abbreviated system. **whether**: if. **he had the story written out**: he asked someone to write it down for him. **handed me**: gave me.
MS: manuscript, original version. **trade secret**: a secret among members of the same profession.

FAITHFUL: true, constant.

lad: boy.

allowed: permitted. **sit up**: stay up *(not go to bed)*.

uttering: pronouncing, producing. **low**: low frequency or low volume. **wail**: cry. **misery**: unhappiness. **disappeared**: went out of sight. **staircase**: set of stairs. **startled**: surprised.

nervous: worried, apprehensive. **on reflection**: after thinking about it. **sinful people**: people who have done bad things. **do harm to**: hurt, damage. **tucked myself up**: got into bed. **the Pater**: father *(old fashioned)*.

It seemed: the story was.
former: previous, preceding. **lessee**: tenant, person who leases or rents a property. **Christian name**: first name.

make his fortune: earn a lot of money.
bush: wild lands in Australia. **few and far between**: very infrequent.

those early days; and, even when one was caught, the portable property found upon the body was often of hardly sufficiently negotiable value to pay the simple funeral expenses rendered necessary. So that it took Johnson nearly twenty years to make his fortune.

The self-imposed task was accomplished at last, however, and then, having successfully eluded the police, and got clear out of the Colony, he returned to England, full of hope and joy, to claim his bride.

He reached the house to find it silent and deserted. All that the neighbours could tell him was that, soon after his own departure, the family had, on one foggy night, unostentatiously disappeared, and that nobody had ever seen or heard anything of them since, although the landlord and most of the local tradesmen had made searching inquiries. Poor Johnson, frenzied with grief, sought his lost love all over the world. But he never found her, and, after years of fruitless effort, he returned to end his lonely life in the very house where, in the happy bygone days, he and his beloved Emily had passed so many blissful hours.

He had lived there quite alone, wandering about the empty rooms, weeping and calling to his Emily to come back to him; and when the poor old fellow died, his ghost still kept the business on.

It was there, the Pater said, when he took the house, and the agent had knocked ten pounds a year off the rent in consequence.

After that, I was continually meeting Johnson about the place at all times of the night, and so, indeed, were we all. We used to walk round it and stand aside to let it pass, at first; but, when we grew more at home with it, and there seemed no necessity for so much ceremony, we used to walk straight through it. You could not say it was ever much in the way.

It was a gentle, harmless, old ghost, too, and we all felt very sorry for it, and pitied it. The women folk, indeed, made quite a pet of it, for a while. Its faithfulness touched them so.

But as time went on, it grew to be a bit of a bore. You see it was full of sadness. There was nothing cheerful or genial about it. You felt sorry for it, but it irritated you. It would sit on the stairs and cry for hours at a stretch; and, whenever we woke up in the night, one was sure to hear it pottering

caught: taken by thieves *(so Johnson was trying to earn money by stealing from other travellers)*. **portable property**: valuables which a traveller carried with him.
hardly sufficiently negotiable value: not worth anything.
rendered: made.
self-imposed task: objective that he had decided. **accomplished**: achieved, finished. **eluded**: avoided, escaped from.
clear out of: away from.
claim his bride: marry the woman promised to him.
reached: arrived at. **deserted**: with nobody there.
neighbours: people living near.
departure: leaving. **foggy**: type of weather when you can't see anything. **unostentatiously**: without any sign.
landlord: owner of the house.
tradesmen: shopkeepers and workers. **searching**: insistent, thorough. **frenzied**: mad, crazy. **grief**: sadness. **sought**: looked for.
fruitless: useless, without result. **lonely**: solitary.
the very house: exactly the house. **bygone**: past. **beloved**: loved one. **blissful**: ecstatic, extremely happy.
quite alone: completely on his own. **wandering**: walking without direction. **weeping**: crying.
fellow: man.
kept the business on: continued to do the same things.
Pater: father.
agent: man responsible for renting the house. **knocked ten pounds a year off the rent**: reduced it by ten pounds a year. **in consequence**: because of this fact. **continually**: all the time.

stand aside: get out of its way.
grew more at home with it: became accustomed to it.

straight through it: directly passing through the ghost's body.
gentle: kind, inoffensive. **harmless**: unable to hurt anyone.

women folk: women *(old-fashioned term)*.
made quite a pet of it: treated it with affection. **for a while**: for a short time. **faithfulness**: its attachment to Emily, its constancy. **touched them**: moved them emotionally. **bore**: boring or monotonous person. **cheerful**: lively, happy. **genial**: happy. **It would sit**: *Note the use of would to indicate past habits*. **at a stretch**: without interruption. **one**: impersonal pronoun. **pottering**: moving.

23

about the passages and in and out of the different rooms, moaning and sighing, so that we could not get to sleep again very easily. And when we had a party on, it would come and sit outside the drawing-room door, and sob all the time. It did not do anybody any harm exactly, but it cast a gloom over the whole affair.

"Oh, I'm getting sick of this old fool," said the Pater, one evening (the Dad can be very blunt, when he is put out, as you know), after Johnson had been more of a nuisance than usual, and had spoiled a good game of whist, by sitting up the chimney and groaning, till nobody knew what were trumps or what suit had been led, even. "We shall have to get rid of him, somehow or other. I wish I knew how to do it."

"Well", said the Mater, "depend upon it, you'll never see the last of him until he's found Emily's grave. That's what he is after. You find Emily's grave, and put him on to that, and he'll stop there. That's the only thing to do. You mark my words."

The idea seemed reasonable, but the difficulty in the way was that we none of us knew where Emily's grave was any more than the ghost of Johnson himself did. The Governor suggested palming off some other Emily's grave upon the poor thing, but, as luck would have it, there did not seem to have been an Emily of any sort buried anywhere for miles round. I never came across a neighbourhood so utterly destitute of dead Emilies.

I thought for a bit, and then I hazarded a suggestion myself. "Couldn't we fake up something for the old chap?" I queried. "He seems a simple-minded old sort. He might take it in. Anyhow, we could but try."

"By Jove, so we will," exclaimed my father; and the very next morning we had the workmen in, and fixed up a little mound at the bottom of the orchard with a tombstone over it, bearing the following inscription:-

Sacred
TO THE MEMORY OF
EMILY
HER LAST WORDS WERE-
'TELL JOHNSON I LOVE HIM'

"That ought to fetch him," mused the Dad as he surveyed the work when finished. "I am sure I hope it does."

moaning: making a crying sound, complaining. **sighing**: expressing regret, sadness.

drawing-room: room used for formal occasions. **sob**: cry.

harm: damage, hurt.

cast a gloom over the whole affair: made the whole party more depressing. **fool**: stupid person.

blunt: direct, rude. **put out**: annoyed, irritated.

nuisance: annoying or irritating person or event.

spoiled: ruined. **whist**: card game.

chimney: above the fireplace where the smoke goes. **groaning**: crying. **trumps**: the most important suit in a game of cards. **suit**: four divisions of a pack of cards: *spades, hearts, diamonds, clubs*.

led: played in a card game. **get rid of him**: dispose of him, remove him. **Mater**: mother *(old fashioned)*.

grave: tomb.

mark my words: be sure of what I say.

reasonable: sensible, plausible.

palming off: substituting.

as luck would have it: by an unfortunate coincidence.

buried: put underground after death.

neighbourhood: vicinity, surroundings.

utterly destitute: completely without.

hazarded a suggestion: made a risky suggestion.

fake: falsify. **chap**: man.

queried: asked. **simple-minded**: not very intelligent.

take it in: believe in it. **we could but try**: we can only try.

By Jove: exclamation, by God.

the very next morning: exactly the next morning. **had the workmen in**: we called the workmen. **fixed up**: constructed.

mound: pile of earth. **orchard**: field of fruit trees. **tombstone**: stone put over a tomb with the name of the dead person. **bearing the following inscription**: with the following written on it. *sacred*: holy, dedicated.

That ought to fetch him: that should bring him here. **mused**: thought. **surveyed**: looked at.

It did!

We lured him down there that very night; and - well, there, it was one of the most pathetic things I have ever seen, the way Johnson sprang upon that tombstone and wept. Dad and old Squibbins, the gardener, cried like children when they saw it.

Johnson has never troubled us any more in the house since then. It spends every night now, sobbing on the grave, and seems quite happy.

"There still?"

Oh yes. I'll take you fellows down and show you it, next time you come to our place: 10 p.m. to 4 a.m. are its general hours, 10 to 2 on Saturdays.

Comprehension Questions

1. What is the "trade secret"?
2. Why is Teddy allowed to stay up late?
3. How does he meet Johnson?
4. How does he first feel?
5. What makes him decide he has nothing to fear?
6. Who does Johnson love?
7. Why can't he marry her?
8. Why does he go to Australia?
9. What is meant by "Australia was not then what it became later on"?
10. How does Johnson try to make his fortune?
11. What is meant by "the portable property found upon the body was often of hardly sufficiently negotiable value to pay the simple funeral expenses rendered necessary"?
12. How long does it take him to make his fortune?
13. What are his feelings on returning to England?
14. What does he find?
15. What has happened to the family?
16. Why do you think "the landlord and most of the local tradesmen had made searching inquiries"?
17. What does Johnson do?
18. Where does he die?
19. How does he spend his last years?
20. Why does the agent "knock ten pounds off the rent"?
21. What do the family do first when they meet the ghost?
22. What is meant by "When we grew more at home with it, and

26

lured: attracted.
pathetic: sad, full of pathos.
sprang: jumped. **wept**: cried.

sobbing: crying.

fellows: men.

---

there seemed no necessity for so much ceremony, we used to walk straight through it"?

23. Why do they all feel sorry for it and pity it at first?
24. Why do the women make "quite a pet of it"?
25. In what way do their feelings change?
26. What is meant by "You felt sorry for it, but it irritated you"?
27. Why does the ghost become a "bit of a bore"?
28. What effect does the ghost's presence have on parties?
29. How does the ghost spoil "a good game of whist"?
30. What do they decide to do?
31. What does Teddy's mother decide the ghost is looking for? What is her advice?
32. What is the difficulty in the way of the plan?
33. What is meant by "The Governor suggested palming off some other Emily's grave upon the poor thing"?
34. What is meant by "I never came across a neighbourhood so utterly destitute of dead Emilies"?
35. What does Teddy suggest they should do?
36. Why does he think the ghost may fall for the trick?
37. What do they do?
38. Where do they put the tombstone?
39. Why do you think they put the words "Tell Johnson I love him" on the tombstone?
40. What does Johnson do when he sees the tombstone?
41. Why do you think "Dad and old Sqibbins cried like children when they saw it"?
42. Has the trick solved their problem?
43. Where and how does Johnson spend his nights?
44. When does the ghost generally appear?

THE DOCTOR'S STORY

It made me cry very much, that story, young Biffles told it with so much feeling. We were all a little thoughtful after it, and I noticed even the old Doctor covertly wipe away a tear. Uncle John brewed another bowl of punch, however, and we gradually grew more resigned.

The Doctor, indeed, after a while became almost cheerful, and told us about the ghost of one of his patients.

I cannot give you his story. I wish I could. They all said afterwards that it was the best of the lot - the most ghastly and terrible - but I could not make any sense of it myself. It seemed so incomplete.

He began all right and then something seemed to happen, and then he was finishing it. I cannot make out what he did with the middle of the story.

It ended up, I know, however, with somebody finding something; and that put Mr Coombes in mind of a very curious affair that took place at an old mill, once kept by his brother-in-law.

Mr Coombes said he would tell us his story, and before anybody could stop him, he had begun.

Mr Coombes said the story was called:-

THE HAUNTED MILL
or
THE RUINED HOME
(Mr Coombes's Story)

Well, you all know my brother-in-law, Mr Parkins (began Mr Coombes, taking the long clay pipe from his mouth, and putting it behind his ear: we did not know his brother-in-law, but we said we did, so as to save time), and you know of course that he once took a lease of an old mill in Surrey, and went to live there.

Now you must know that, years ago, this very mill had been occupied by a wicked old miser, who died there, leaving - so it was rumoured - all his money hidden somewhere about the place. Naturally enough, every one who had since come to live at the mill had tried to find the treasure; but none had ever succeeded, and the local wiseacres said

covertly: secretly.
wipe away a tear: clean a tear from his eye.
gradually: a little at a time. **grew**: became. **resigned**: fatalistic.
cheerful: happy.

the best of the lot: the best of all of them. **ghastly**: frightening.

incomplete: unfinished.

make out: understand, calculate.

ended up: finished.
put Mr Coombes in mind of: made Mr Coombes remember.
curious: strange. **affair**: event. **took place**: happened. **mill**: place
where flour is made. **brother-in-law**: brother of his wife or his
sister's husband.

HAUNTED: infested with ghosts.

RUINED: destroyed.

clay: made of earth.

lease: rent.

wicked: bad. **miser**: person who cares only about money.
so it was rumoured: so people said. **hidden**: concealed, put in
a secret place.

succeeded: had success. **wiseacres**: *(ironic)* intelligent people.

that nobody ever would, unless the ghost of the miserly miller should, one day, take a fancy to one of the tenants, and disclose to him the secret of the hiding-place.

My brother-in-law did not attach much importance to the story, regarding it as an old woman's tale, and, unlike his predecessors, made no attempt whatever to discover the hidden gold.

"Unless business was very different then from what it is now," said my brother-in-law, "I don't see how a miller could very well have saved anything, however much of a miser he might have been: at all events, not enough to make it worth the trouble of looking for it."

Still, he could not altogether get rid of the idea of that treasure. One night he went to bed. There was nothing very extraordinary about that, I admit. He often did go to bed of a night. What *was* remarkable, however, was that exactly as the clock of the village church chimed the last stroke of twelve, my brother-in-law woke up with a start, and felt himself quite unable to go to sleep again.

Joe (his Christian name was Joe) sat up in bed, and looked around.

At the foot of the bed something stood very still, wrapped in shadow.

It moved into the moonlight, and then my brother-in-law saw that it was the figure of a wizened little old man, in knee-breeches and a pig-tail.

In an instant the story of the hidden treasure and the old miser flashed across his mind.

"He's come to show me where it's hid," thought my brother-in-law; and he resolved that he would not spend all this money on himself, but would devote a small percentage of it towards doing good to others.

The apparition moved towards the door: my brother-in-law put on his trousers and followed it. The ghost went downstairs into the kitchen, glided over and stood in front of the hearth, sighed and disappeared.

Next morning, Joe had a couple of bricklayers in, and made them haul out the stove and pull down the chimney, while he stood behind with a potato-sack in which to put the gold. They knocked down half the wall, and never found so much as a fourpenny bit. My brother-in-law did not know what to think.

miserly: mean. **miller**: man making flour at the mill. **take a fancy to**: become friendly with. **tenants**: people renting a property. **disclose**: tell.

regarding: thinking of. **old woman's tale**: untrue or exaggerated story. **unlike**: not like, different from. **predecessors**: people who had rented the mill before. **discover**: find. **Unless**: if not.

saved: reserved money for the future.
at all events: in any case.
worth the trouble: repay the difficulties.
altogether: completely. **get rid of**: forget about.

extraordinary: unusual.
remarkable: surprising.
chimed: sounded. **stroke**: single sound of bell.
with a start: suddenly.
quite unable: completely unable.

still: stationary. **wrapped**: covered.

figure: shape. **wizened**: with lines caused by age.
knee-breeches: old fashioned trousers ending at the knee. **pig-tail**: hair tied at the back of the neck. **instant**: moment. **hidden**: concealed. **miser**: person interested only in money.

resolved: decided.
devote: dedicate.
percentage: proportion.
apparition: ghost.

glided: moved without touching the ground.
hearth: fireplace. **sighed**: made a sad sound. **disappeared**: became invisible. **had a couple of bricklayers in**: called two workers to look behind the fireplace. *Note the passive construction.* **haul out**: pull out. **stove**: oven, where the cooking was done. **chimney**: area above fireplace. **gold**: money. **knocked down**: demolished. **never found so much as**: didn't even find. **a fourpenny bit**: a coin of the value of four pence (which doesn't exist).

31

The next night the old man appeared again, and again led the way into the kitchen. This time, however, instead of going to the fireplace, it stood more in the middle of the room, and sighed there.

"Oh, I see what he means now," said my brother-in-law to himself; "it's under the floor. Why did the old idiot go and stand up against the stove, so as to make me think it was up the chimney?"

They spent the next day in taking up the kitchen floor; but the only thing they found was a three-pronged fork, and the handle of that was broken.

On the third night, the ghost reappeared, quite unabashed, and for a third time made for the kitchen. Arriving there, it looked up at the ceiling and vanished.

"Umph! he don't seem to have learned much sense where he's been to," muttered Joe, as he trotted back to bed; "I should have thought he might have done that at first."

Still, there seemed to be no doubt now where the treasure lay, and the first thing after breakfast they started pulling down the ceiling. They got every inch of the ceiling down, and they took up the boards of the room above.

They discovered about as much treasure as you would expect to find in an empty quart-pot.

On the fourth night, when the ghost appeared, as usual, my brother-in-law was so wild that he threw his boots at it; and the boots passed through the body, and broke a looking-glass.

On the fifth night, when Joe awoke, as he always did now at twelve, the ghost was standing in a dejected attitude, looking very miserable. There was an appealing look in its large sad eyes that quite touched my brother-in-law.

"After all," he thought, "perhaps the silly chap's doing his best. Maybe he has forgotten where he really did put it, and is trying to remember. I'll give him another chance."

The ghost appeared grateful and delighted at seeing Joe prepare to follow him, and led the way into the attic, pointed to the ceiling, and vanished.

"Well, he's hit it this time, I do hope," said my brother-in-law; and next day they set to work to take the roof off the place.

It took them three days to get the roof thoroughly off, and all they found was a bird's nest; after securing which they covered up the house with tarpaulins, to keep it dry.

You might have thought that would have cured the poor

led the way: showed the way. **however**: on the other hand.

sighed: cried.

stove: cooker.

three-pronged: with three points.
handle: part of fork which you hold it with.
unabashed: not embarrassed.
made for: moved towards.
ceiling: area above the room. **vanished**: became invisible.
Umph!: expression of irritation. **he don't seem**: *(dialect)* he doesn't seem. **muttered**: said in an indistinct voice. **trotted**: walked quickly and lightly.

where the treasure lay: where the money was. **the first thing after**: immediately after. **ceiling**: area above a room. **every inch**: all. **boards**: wood under the floor.
discovered: found.
empty quart-pot: receptacle of capacity two pints, but containing nothing.
wild: angry.
looking-glass: mirror.

dejected: depressed. **attitude**: position, pose.
miserable: sad. **appealing**: attractive.
touched: moved emotionally.
silly: stupid. **chap**: man.

grateful: full of thanks. **delighted**: very happy.
attic: room at the top of a house.
pointed to: indicated. **vanished**: disappeared.
hit it: got it right.
set to work: started work.
thoroughly: completely.
nest: structure built by birds. **securing**: making safe.
tarpaulins: large waterproof cloths.

fellow of looking for treasure. But it didn't.

He said there must be something in it all, or the ghost would never keep on coming as it did; and that, having gone so far, he would go on to the end, and solve the mystery, cost what it might.

Night after night, he would get out of his bed and follow that spectral old fraud about the house. Each night, the old man would indicate a different place; and, on each following day, my brother-in-law would proceed to break up the mill at the point indicated, and look for the treasure. At the end of three weeks, there was not a room in the mill fit to live in. Every wall had been pulled down, every floor had been taken up, every ceiling had had a hole knocked in it. And then, as suddenly as they had begun, the ghost's visits ceased; and my brother-in-law was left in peace, to rebuild the place at his leisure.

"What induced the old image to play such a silly trick upon a family man and a ratepayer?" Ah! that's just what I cannot tell you.

Some said that the ghost of the wicked old man had done it to punish my brother-in-law for not believing in him at first; while others held that the apparition was probably that of some deceased local plumber and glazier, who would naturally take an interest in seeing a house knocked about and spoilt. But nobody knew anything for certain.

Comprehension Questions

1. Why can't the writer tell the Doctor's ghost story?
2. What reminds Mr Coombes of his brother-in-law's ghost?
3. What is meant by "we did not know his brother-in-law, but we said we did, so as to save time"?
4. What is the "rumour" about the old mill?
5. What does everyone who leases the mill try to do?
6. What do the "local wiseacres" say is the only way the miser's treasure would be found?
7. Why doesn't his brother-in-law take much notice of the story?
8. Why does he think the miser could not have saved much money?
9. What is meant by "not enough to make it worth the trouble of looking for it"?
10. What happens to Joe one night at midnight?
11. What does he see?

34

cost what it might: however much it cost.

spectral: ghostly. **fraud**: false person.

fit: suitable.

ceased: stopped.
at his leisure: in his own time.
induced: made. **silly**: stupid. **trick**: joke.
ratepayer: honest man who paid local taxes.

wicked: unkind, bad.

held: thought, sustained. **apparition**: ghost.
deceased: dead. **plumber**: man working with hydraulic system
in house. **glazier**: man working with glass.
spoilt: ruined, destroyed.

---

12. What does he immediately think of, as soon as he sees the
    ghost?
13. What do the ghost and Joe do?
14. What does Joe do the next morning? What is the result?
15. In what state is the kitchen after three such days and nights?
16. What happens on the fouth night? Why?
17. Why does he decide to follow the ghost again on the fifth night?
18. What do they find when they take the roof off?
19. What is meant by "You might have thought that would have
    cured the poor fellow of looking for treasure"? Does it?
20. Why does he continue?
21. What is the mill like after three weeks?
22. What happens afterwards?
23. Why do some say the ghost played such a trick?
24. Why would the ghost of some deceased plumber or glazier
    want to see a house knocked down?

INTERLUDE

We had some more punch, and then the curate told us a story. I could not make head or tail of the curate's story, so I cannot retail it to you. We none of us could make head or tail of that story. It was a good story enough, so far as material went. There seemed to be an enormous amount of plot, and enough incident to have made a dozen novels. I never before heard a story containing so much incident, nor one dealing with so many varied characters.

I should say that every human being our curate had ever known or met, or heard of, was brought into that story. There were simply hundreds of them. Every five seconds he would introduce into the tale a completely fresh collection of characters accompanied by a brand new set of incidents.

This was the sort of story it was:-

"Well, then, my uncle went into the garden, and got his gun, but, of course, it wasn't there, and Scroggins said he didn't believe it."

"Didn't believe what? Who's Scroggins?"

"Scroggins! Oh, why he was the other man, you know - it was his wife."

"*What* was his wife - what's *she* got to do with it?"

"Why, that's what I'm telling you. It was she that found the hat. She'd come up with her cousin to London - her cousin was my sister-in-law, and the other niece had married a man named Evans, and Evans, after it was all over, had taken the box round to Mr Jacobs', because Jacobs' father had seen the man, when he was alive, and when he was dead, Joseph—"

"Now look here, never you mind Evans and the box; what's become of your uncle and the gun?"

"The gun! What gun?"

"Why, the gun that your uncle used to keep in the garden, and that wasn't there. What did he do with it? Did he kill any of these people with it - these Jacobses and Evanses and Scrogginses and Josephses? Because, if so, it was a good and useful work, and we should enjoy hearing about it."

"No - oh no - how could he? - he had been built up alive in the wall, you know, and when Edward IV spoke to the abbot about it, my sister said that in her then state of health

36

curate: priest.
retail: communicate.
make head or tail of: understand at all.
amount: quantity.
plot: story. **dozen**: twelve.

dealing with: involving.

tale: story.
brand new: completely new.

niece: daughter of brother or sister.
over: finished.

never you mind: don't tell us about.
become of: happened to.

Why: *here used as an exclamation.*

built up alive: closed behind a wall while still alive.

abbot: important religious official, head of abbey. **her then state of health**: her physical condition then.

she could not and would not, as it was endangering the child's life. So they christened it Horatio, after her own son, who had been killed at Waterloo before he was born, and Lord Napier himself said—"

"Look here, do you know what you are talking about?" we asked him at this point.

He said "No," but he knew it was every word of it true, because his aunt had seen it herself. Whereupon we covered him over with the tablecloth, and he went to sleep.

And then Uncle told us a story.

Uncle said his was a real story.

THE GHOST OF THE BLUE CHAMBER
(My Uncle's Story)

I don't want to make you fellows nervous, began my uncle in a peculiarly impressive, not to say blood-curdling, tone of voice, "and if you would rather that I did not mention it, I won't; but, as a matter of fact, this very house, in which we are now sitting, is haunted."

"You don't say that!" exclaimed Mr Coombes.

"What's the use of your saying I don't say it when I have just said it?" retorted my uncle somewhat pettishly. "You do talk so foolishly. I tell you the house is haunted. Regularly on Christmas Eve the Blue Chamber [they called the room next to the nursery the "blue chamber", at my uncle's, most of the toilet service being of that shade] is haunted by the ghost of a sinful man - a man who once killed a Christmas wait with a lump of coal."

"How did he do it?" asked Mr Coombes, with eager anxiousness. "Was it difficult?"

"I do not know how he did it," replied my uncle; "he did not explain the process. The wait had taken up a position just inside the front gate, and was singing a ballad. It is presumed that, when he opened his mouth for B flat, the lump of coal was thrown by the sinful man from one of the windows, and that it went down the wait's throat and choked him."

"You want to be a good shot, but it is certainly worth trying," murmured Mr Coombes thoughtfully.

"But that was not his only crime, alas!" added my uncle.

38

she could not and would not: *Note the verb is missing so this is nonsense*. **endangering**: putting into danger. **christened**: baptized. **Waterloo**: famous battle in 1815.

Whereupon: at this point in time.
tablecloth: cloth put over table at dinner.

fellows: men.
peculiarly: strangely. **blood-curdling**: extremely frightening.
would rather: would prefer.
as a matter of fact: in fact.
haunted: infested with ghosts.
you don't say that!: really?

retorted: replied, answered. **pettishly**: in an irritated way.
foolishly: stupidly.

nursery: room for children.
toilet service: articles in bathroom.
sinful: bad.
wait: street singer at Christmas time. **lump**: piece. **coal**: solid black fuel. **eager**: keen, enthusiastic.
anxiousness: worried state.

gate: external door onto the street. **ballad**: slow song.
B flat: musical note.

throat: passage between mouth and stomach where food and air pass. **choked**: suffocated. **You want to be**: you need to be. **a good shot**: someone who hits his target. **worth trying**: justifies the attempt. **alas**: expression of regret, sadness.

"Prior to that he had killed a solo cornet-player."

"No! Is that really a fact?" exclaimed Mr Coombes.

"Of course it's a fact," answered my uncle testily; "at all events, as much a fact as you can expect to get in a case of this sort.

"How very captious you are this evening. The circumstantial evidence was overwhelming. The poor fellow, the cornet-player, had been in the neighbourhood barely a month. Old Mr Bishop, who kept the 'Jolly Sand Boys' at the time, and from whom I had the story, said he had never known a more hard-working and energetic solo cornet-player. He, the cornet-player, only knew two tunes, but Mr Bishop said that the man could not have played with more vigour, or for more hours a day, if he had known forty. The two tunes he did play were 'Annie Laurie' and 'Home, Sweet Home'; and as regards his performance of the former melody, Mr Bishop said that a mere child could have told what it was meant for.

"This musician - this poor, friendless artist used to come regularly and play in this street just opposite for two hours every evening. One evening he was seen, evidently in response to an invitation, going into this very house, *but was never seen coming out of it!*"

"Did the townsfolk try offering any reward for his recovery?" asked Mr Coombes.

"Not a ha'penny," replied my uncle.

"Another summer," continued my uncle, "a German band visited here, intending - so they announced on their arrival - to stay till the autumn.

"On the second day from their arrival, the whole company, as fine and healthy a body of men as one could wish to see, were invited to dinner by this sinful man, and, after spending the whole of the next twenty-four hours in bed, left the town a broken and dyspeptic crew; the parish doctor, who had attended them, giving it as his opinion that it was doubtful if they would, any of them, be fit to play an air again."

"You - you don't know the recipe, do you?" asked Mr Coombes.

"Unfortunately I do not," replied my uncle; "but the chief ingredient was said to have been railway refreshment-room pork-pie.

"I forget the man's other crimes," my uncle went on; "I used to know them all at one time, but my memory is not

Prior to: before. **cornet**: musical instrument like a trumpet.

testily: in an irritated way.
at all events: anyway.

captious: annoying.
circumstantial evidence: indirect proof. **overwhelming**: very substantial. **fellow**: man. **neighbourhood**: area, district.
barely a month: only just a month. **'Jolly Sand Boys'**: name of pub.

tunes: melodies.
vigour: force.

performance: execution. **former**: first.
mere: simple.
friendless: without friends.

evidently: obviously.
townsfolk: people from the town. **reward**: financial incentive.

recovery: finding him again.
not a ha' penny: not even half a penny, no money at all.

healthy: in good physical condition. **body**: group.
sinful: bad.
the whole of: all of.
dyspeptic: with problems of digestion. **crew**: group of men.
parish: area under the authority of the church. **attended**: visited.
doubtful: dubious. **be fit**: be able. **air**: melody.
recipe: instructions for cooking a particular dish.

chief: main.

pork-pie: meat pie often sold at stations and other places.

what it was. I do not, however, believe I am doing his memory an injustice in believing that he was not entirely unconnected with the death, and subsequent burial, of a gentleman who used to play the harp with his toes; and that neither was he altogether unresponsible for the lonely grave of an unknown stranger who had once visited the neighbourhood, an Italian peasant lad, a performer upon the barrel-organ.

"Every Christmas Eve," said my uncle, cleaving with low impressive tones the strange awed silence that, like a shadow, seemed to have slowly stolen into and settled down upon the room, "the ghost of this sinful man haunts the Blue Chamber, in this very house. There, from midnight until cock-crow, amid wild muffled shrieks and groans and mocking laughter and the ghostly sound of horrid blows, it does fierce phantom fight with the spirits of the solo cornet-player and the murdered wait, assisted at intervals by the shades of the German band; while the ghost of the strangled harpist plays mad ghostly melodies with ghostly toes on the ghost of a broken harp."

Uncle said the Blue Chamber was comparatively useless as a sleeping-apartment on Christmas Eve.

"Hark!" said my uncle, raising a warning hand towards the ceiling, while we held our breath, and listened; "Hark! I believe they are at it now - in the *Blue Chamber*!"

I rose up, and said that *I* would sleep in the Blue Chamber. Before I tell you my own story, however - the story of what happened in the Blue Chamber - I would wish to preface it with:-

---

Comprehension Questions

1. Why can't he tell the curate's story?
2. What is meant by "enough incident to have made a dozen novels"?
3. Why does he say that "every human being our curate had ever known or met, or heard of, was brought into that story"?
4. What is the connection between Scroggins and Evans?
5. Why do you think they say that if the curate's uncle has killed any of the Jacobses, Evanses, Scrogginses or Josephses they will enjoy hearing about it?
6. What do they do to keep the curate quiet?
7. Why is his uncle frightened of making them nervous?
8. Whose ghost haunts the house? How does he kill the wait?
9. Who else does he kill?

subsequent: later. **burial**: putting a dead body underground.
harp: musical instrument with many strings.
altogether: completely. **lonely**: solitary.
grave: tomb, death.
neighbourhood: area, vicinity. **peasant**: farm worker. **lad**: boy.
performer: player. **barrel-organ**: musical instrument often played in the street. **cleaving**: cutting.
awed: respectful.
stolen into: come quietly.
settled down: rested. **sinful**: bad, evil. **haunts**: infests.

cock-crow: dawn, when the cock sings. **amid**: in the middle of.
muffled: heard from a distance. **shrieks**: cries. **groans**: cries.
mocking: sarcastic. **blows**: a fight. **fierce**: wild, savage.
phantom: ghost. **wait**: street singer or musician at Christmas time. **shades**: ghosts.
harpist: musician playing the harp.
toes: extremities of foot.
comparatively: relatively.

Hark: listen. **raising**: moving up. **warning**: informing of danger.
ceiling: upper part of a room. **held our breath**: did not breathe out. **at it**: fighting.
rose up: got up.

preface: precede.

---

10. What kind of musician is the solo cornet-player?
11. What is meant by "the man could not have played with more vigour, or for more hours a day, if he had known forty"?
12. What happens to the German band?
13. What is the chief ingredient of the dinner which makes them so ill? What does this suggest about railway refreshment rooms?
14. Why do you think Mr Coombes is so interested in the methods used to eliminate these musicians?
15. What other two deaths is the man suspected of?
16. What have all the murdered people in common?
17. What happens every Christmas Eve?
18. What kind of sounds are heard from the Blue Chamber on that night?
19. What does the writer decide to do?

A PERSONAL EXPLANATION

I feel a good deal of hesitation about telling you this story of my own. You see it is not a story like the other stories that I have been telling you, or rather that Teddy Biffles, Mr Coombes, and my uncle have been telling you: it is a true story. It is not a story told by a person sitting round a fire on Christmas Eve, drinking whisky punch: it is a record of events that actually happened.

Indeed, it is not a "story" at all, in the commonly accepted meaning of the word: it is a report. It is, I feel, almost out of place in a book of this kind. It is more suitable to a biography, or an English history.

There is another thing that makes it difficult for me to tell you this story, and that is, that it is all about myself. In telling you this story, I shall have to keep on talking about myself; and talking about ourselves is what we modern-day authors have a strong objection to doing. If we literary men of the new school have one praiseworthy yearning more ever present to our minds than another it is the yearning never to appear in the slightest degree egotistical. I myself, so I am told, carry this coyness - this shrinking reticence concerning anything connected with my own personality, almost too far; and people grumble at me because of it. People come to me and say:-

"Well, now, why don't you talk about yourself a bit? That's what we want to read about. Tell us something about yourself."

But I have always replied, "No." It is not that I do not think the subject an interesting one. I cannot myself conceive of any topic more likely to prove fascinating to the world as a whole, or at all events to the cultured portion of it. But I will not do it, on principle. It is inartistic, and it sets a bad example to the younger men. Other writers (a few of them) do it, I know; but I will not - not as a rule.

Under ordinary circumstances, therefore, I should not tell you this story at all. I should say to myself, "No! It is a good story, it is a moral story, it is a strange, weird, enthralling sort of a story; and the public, I know, would like to hear it; and I should like to tell it to them; but it is all about myself - about what I said, and what I saw, and what I did, and I

44

a good deal of: a lot of.

record: account.
actually: really.
commonly: widely.

suitable: appropriate.
biography: true story of someone's life.

praiseworthy: good, virtuous. **yearning**: desire.
ever present: always in.
slightest: smallest. **degree**: way. **egotistical**: concerned only
with oneself. **so I am told**: as people tell me. *Note the passive
construction*. **coyness**: shy nature. **shrinking**: timid, frightened.
reticence: not wanting to talk about oneself. **grumble**: complain.

conceive: think, imagine.
topic: subject. **likely**: probable. **prove**: be. **fascinating**:
interesting. **at all events**: in any case. **portion**: part.

sets a bad example: leads into bad habits.
as a rule: usually.
therefore: so.

weird: mysterious. **enthralling**: exciting.

cannot do it. My retiring, anti-egotistical nature will not
permit me to talk in this way about myself."

But the circumstances surrounding this story are not ordinary,
and there are reasons prompting me, in spite of my modesty,
to rather welcome the opportunity of relating it.

As I stated at the beginning, there has been unpleasantness
in our family over this party of ours, and, as regards myself
in particular, and my share in the events I am now about to
set forth, gross injustice has been done me.

As a means of replacing my character in its proper light -
of dispelling the clouds of calumny and misconception
with which it has been darkened, I feel that my best course
is to give a simple, dignified narration of the plain facts, and
allow the unprejudiced to judge for themselves. My chief
object, I candidly confess, is to clear myself from unjust
aspersion. Spurred by this motive - and I think it is an
honourable and a right motive - I find I am enabled to
overcome my usual repugnance to talking about myself,
and can thus tell:-

MY OWN STORY

As soon my uncle had finished his story, I, as I have already
told you, rose up and said that *I* would sleep in the Blue
Chamber that very night.

"Never!" cried my uncle, springing up. "You shall not put
yourself in this deadly peril. Besides, the bed is not made."

"Never mind the bed," I replied. "I have lived in furnished
apartments for gentlemen, and have been accustomed to
sleep on beds that have never been made from one year's
end to the other. Do not thwart me in my resolve. I am
young, and have had a clear conscience now for over a
month. The spirits will not harm me. I may even do them
some little good, and induce them to be quiet and go away.
Besides, I should like to see the show."

Saying which, I sat down again. (How Mr Coombes came
to be in my chair, instead of at the other side of the room,
where he had been all the evening; and why he never
offered to apologize when I sat right down on top of him;
and why young Biffles should have tried to palm himself
off upon me as my Uncle John, and induced me, under that

retiring: shy. **anti-egotistical**: altruistic.

surrounding: concerning.
prompting: stimulating.
modesty: shy nature. **relating**: telling.

stated: said.

share: part.
set forth: write down. **gross injustice**: great wrong.

dispelling: making invisible. **calumny**: lies told to hurt others.
misconception: misunderstanding, wrong impression. **darke-ned**: made dark. **plain**: simple, unadorned.
unprejudiced: with no prejudice. **judge**: decide.
candidly: honestly. **clear myself**: show my innocence.
unjust: unfair. **aspersion**: criticism, insult. **Spurred**: stimulated.
I am enabled to: I can.
overcome: conquer. **repugnance**: disgust.
thus: in this way.

rose up: got up.

springing: jumping.
deadly: fatal. **peril**: danger. **Besides**: in addition. **made**: prepared. **Never mind**: it doesn't matter. **furnished**: with fur-niture and decorations included. **accustomed**: used.

thwart: prevent. **resolve**: decision.

harm: hurt.
induce: make.

apologize: say sorry. **right**: exactly.

palm himself off: pretend to be.

erroneous impression, to shake him by the hand for nearly three minutes, and tell him that I had always regarded him as father - are matters that, to this day, I have never been able to fully understand.)

They tried to dissuade me from what they termed my foolhardy enterprise, but I remained firm, and claimed my privilege. I was "the guest". "The guest" always sleeps in the haunted chamber on Christmas Eve; it is his perquisite. They said that if I put it on that footing, they had, of course, no answer; and they lighted a candle for me, and accompanied me upstairs in a body.

Whether elevated by the feeling that I was doing a noble action, or animated by a mere general consciousness of rectitude, is not for me to say, but I went upstairs that night with remarkable buoyancy. It was as much as I could do to stop at the landing when I came to it; I felt I wanted to go on up to the roof. But, with the help of the banisters, I restrained my ambition, wished them all good-night, and went in and shut the door.

Things began to go wrong with me from the very first. The candle tumbled out of the candlestick before my hand was off the lock. It kept on tumbling out of the candlestick, and every time I picked it up and put it in, it tumbled out again: I never saw such a slippery candle. I gave up attempting to use the candlestick at last, and carried the candle about in my hand; and, even then, it would not keep upright. So I got wild and threw it out of the window, and undressed and went to bed in the dark.

I did not go to sleep - I did not feel sleepy at all - I lay on my back, looking up at the ceiling, and thinking of things. I wish I could remember some of the ideas that came to me as I lay there, because they were so amusing. I laughed at them myself till the bed shook.

I had been lying like this for half an hour or so, and had forgotten all about the ghost, when, on casually casting my eyes round the room, I noticed for the first time a singularly contented-looking phantom, sitting in the easy-chair by the fire, smoking the ghost of a long clay pipe.

I fancied for the moment, as most people would under similar circumstances, that I must be dreaming. I sat up, and rubbed my eyes.

No! It was a ghost, clear enough. I could see the back of the

erroneous impression: mistake.

matters: affairs, things.

dissuade: persuade not to. **termed**: called.
foolhardy: stupid and risky. **enterprise**: action. **firm**: rigid, unchanging. **claimed**: took. **guest**: person who receives hospitality. **haunted**: infested by ghosts. **chamber**: room. **perquisite**: right. **on that footing**: on that level, in that way.

in a body: all together.

rectitude: being right and good.
remarkable: surprising. **buoyancy**: high spirits, good feeling.
landing: space at the top of the stairs.
banisters: support at the side of the stairs.
restrained: controlled.

tumbled: fell. **candlestick**: support for candle.
lock: mechanism to shut door. **kept on**: continued to.
picked it up: took it from the floor.
slippery: difficult to keep still. **gave up**: stopped.

upright: vertical.
wild: angry. **undressed**: took my clothes off.

amusing: funny.
shook: vibrated.

casually: by chance. **casting**: moving.
singularly: strangely.
contented: happy. **phantom**: ghost. **easy-chair**: armchair.
clay: made of earth.
fancied: imagined.

rubbed: touched.

chair through his body. He looked over towards me, took the shadowy pipe from his lips, and nodded.

The most surprising part of the whole thing to me was that I did not feel in the least alarmed. If anything, I was rather pleased to see him. It was company.

I said, "Good evening. It's been a cold day!"

He said he had not noticed it himself, but dared say I was right.

We remained silent for a few seconds, and then, wishing to put it pleasantly, I said, "I believe I have the honour of addressing the ghost of the gentleman who had the accident with the wait?"

He smiled, and said it was very good of me to remember it. One wait was not much to boast of, but still, every little helped.

I was somewhat staggered at his answer. I had expected a groan of remorse. The ghost appeared, on the contrary, to be rather conceited over the business. I thought that, as he had taken my reference to the wait so quietly, perhaps he would not be offended if I questioned him about the organ-grinder. I felt curious about that poor boy.

"Is it true," I asked, "that you had a hand in the death of that Italian peasant lad who came to the town once with a barrel-organ that played nothing but Scotch airs?"

He quite fired up. "Had a hand in it!" he exclaimed indignantly. "Who has dared to pretend that he assisted me? I murdered the youth myself. Nobody helped me. Alone I did it. Show me the man who says I didn't."

I calmed him. I assured him that I had never, in my own mind, doubted that he was the real and only assassin, and I went on and asked him what he had done with the body of the cornet-player he had killed.

He said, "To which one may you be alluding?"

"Oh, were there any more then?" I inquired.

He smiled, and gave a little cough. He said he did not like to appear to be boasting, but that, counting trombones, there were seven.

"Dear me!" I replied, "you must have had quite a busy time of it, one way and another."

He said that perhaps he ought not to be the one to say so, but that really, speaking of ordinary middle-class society, he thought there were few ghosts who could look back upon a life of more sustained usefulness.

shadowy: ghostly. **nodded**: moved his head in sign of recognition.
in the least: at all. **alarmed**: afraid. **rather**: quite.

dared say: thought.

put it: express it.
addressing: talking to.
wait: Christmas singer/musician.

boast of: talk of with pride or honour.

somewhat staggered: quite surprised.
groan: low cry. **remorse**: regret, penitence. **on the contrary**: with the opposite effect. **conceited**: proud, arrogant.

organ-grinder: street musician who turns the handle on the barrel-organ. **hand**: part.
lad: boy.
Scotch: from Scotland. **airs**: melodies.
fired up: became angry and red.
indignantly: angrily. **assisted**: helped.
youth: young person.

assured: promised.
doubted: had any doubts.

cornet: instrument like a trumpet.
alluding: referring.
inquired: asked.
cough: noise in throat.
boasting: speaking with pride about himself. **trombones**: musical instruments.

ought not to: should not.

sustained: constant. **usefulness**: utility.

He puffed away in silence for a few seconds, while I sat watching him. I had never seen a ghost smoking a pipe before, that I could remember, and it interested me.

I asked him what tobacco he used, and he replied, "The ghost of cut cavendish, as a rule."

He explained that the ghost of all the tobacco that a man smoked in life belonged to him when he became dead. He said he himself had smoked a good deal of cut cavendish when he was alive, so that he was well supplied with the ghost of it now.

I observed that it was a useful thing to know that, and I made up my mind to smoke as much tobacco as ever I could before I died.

I thought I might as well start at once, so I said I would join him in a pipe, and he said, "Do, old man"; and I reached over and got out the necessary paraphernalia from my coat pocket and lit up.

We grew quite chummy after that, and he told me all his crimes. He said he had lived next door once to a young lady who was learning to play the guitar, while a gentleman who practised on the bass-viol lived opposite. And he, with fiendish cunning, had introduced these two unsuspecting young people to one another, and had persuaded them to elope with each other against their parents' wishes, and take their musical instruments with them; and they had done so, and, before the honeymoon was over, *she* had broken his head with the bass-viol, and *he* had tried to cram the guitar down her throat, and had injured her for life.

My friend said he used to lure muffin-men into the passage and then stuff them with their own wares till they burst and died. He said he had quieted eighteen that way.

Young men and women who recited long and dreary poems at evening parties, and callow youths who walked about the streets late at night, playing concertinas, he used to get together and poison in batches of ten, so as to save expense; and park orators and temperance lecturers he used to shut up six in a small room with a glass of water and a collection-box apiece, and let them talk each other to death. It did one good to listen to him.

I asked him when he expected the other ghosts - the ghosts of the wait and the cornet-player, and the German band that Uncle John had mentioned. He smiled, and said they would

puffed: smoked.

cut cavendish: a variety of tobacco.

belonged to him: was his.
a good deal of: a lot of.
well supplied: he had a lot.

made up my mind: decided.

I might as well: it would not be a bad idea if I. **at once**: immediately.
old man: term of affection.
paraphernalia: equipment.
lit up: lit the pipe.
grew: became. **chummy**: friendly.

bass-viol: large stringed instrument of the violin family.
fiendish: devilish. **cunning**: art.

elope: run away to get married.

honeymoon: holiday after two people get married.
cram: push.
injured: damaged.
lure: attract. **muffin-men**: men selling breakfast cakes in the street. **stuff**: fill. **wares**: produce, articles being sold. **burst**: exploded. **quieted**: killed, silenced.
dreary: depressing.
callow: inexperienced. **youths**: young people.
concertinas: musical instruments.
batches: groups.
orators: people who make formal speeches. **temperance**: anti-alcohol. **lecturers**: public speakers.
apiece: each.

never come again, any of them. I said, "Why; isn't it true, then, that they meet you here every Christmas Eve for a row?"

He replied that it *was* true. Every Christmas Eve, for twenty-five years, had he and they fought in that room; but they would never trouble him nor anybody else again. One by one, had he laid them out, spoilt, and utterly useless for all haunting purposes. He had finished off the last German-band ghost that very evening, just before I came upstairs, and had thrown what was left of it out through the slit between the window-sashes. He said it would never be worth calling a ghost again.

"I suppose you will still come yourself, as usual?" I said. "They would be sorry to miss you, I know."

"Oh, I don't know," he replied; "there's nothing much to come for now. Unless," he added kindly, "*you* are going to be here. I'll come if you will sleep here next Christmas Eve."

"I have taken a liking to you," he continued; "you don't fly off, screeching, when you see a party, and your hair doesn't stand on end. You've no idea," he said, "how sick I am of seeing people's hair standing on end."

He said it irritated him. Just then a slight noise reached us from the yard below, and he started and turned deathly black.

"You are ill," I cried, springing towards him; "tell me the best thing to do for you. Shall I drink some brandy, and give you the ghost of it?"

He remained silent, listening intently for a moment, and then he gave a sigh of relief, and the shade came back to his cheek.

"It's all right, "he murmured; "I was afraid it was the cock."

"Oh, it's too early for that," I said. "Why, it's only the middle of the night."

"Oh, that doesn't make any difference to those cursed chickens," he replied bitterly. "They would just as soon crow in the middle of the night as at any other time - sooner, if they thought it would spoil a chap's evening out. I believe they do it on purpose."

He said a friend of his, the ghost of a man who had killed a water-rate collector, used to haunt a house in Long Acre, where they kept fowls in the cellar, and every time a policeman went by and flashed his bull's-eye down the grating, the old cock there would fancy it was the sun, and start crowing like mad; when, of course, the poor ghost had to dissolve, and it would, in consequence get back home sometimes as early as

row: fight.

laid them out: knocked them out. **spoilt**: ruined, destroyed.
utterly: completely.
very: same.
slit: opening.
window-sashes: support for window.

fly off: run away. **screeching**: screaming.
sick: tired.
slight: small.
yard: courtyard, open space inside a building.
deathly black: as black as death.
springing: jumping.

intently: carefully.
sigh of relief: sound when danger has passed. **shade**: shadow.
cheek: side of face. *Note the parody of normal people who
become deathly white and then the colour comes back into their
cheek.* **murmured**: said in an indistinct voice. **cock**: bird that
announces dawn. **cursed**: damned.
bitterly: acidly.
crow: noise of cock.
spoil: ruin. **chap**: man.
on purpose: deliberately, intentionally.

water-rate collector: official who collects local taxes on water.
Long Acre: street in London. **fowls**: chickens. **cellar**: underground store-room. **bull's-eye**: lantern, lamp.
grating: grille. **fancy**: imagine. **crowing**: singing. **like mad**: very
loud. **dissolve**: disappear.

one o'clock in the morning, swearing fearfully because it had only been out for an hour. I agreed that it seemed very unfair. "Oh, it's an absurd arrangement altogether," he continued, quite angrily. "I can't imagine what our old man could have been thinking of when he made it. As I have said to him, over and over again, 'Have a fixed time, and let everybody stick to it - say four o'clock in summer, and six in winter. Then one would know what one was about.'"

"How do you manage when there isn't any cock handy?" I inquired.

He was on the point of replying, when again he started and listened. This time I distinctly heard Mr Bowles's cock, next door, crow twice.

"There you are," he said, rising and reaching for his hat; "that's the sort of thing we have to put up with. What *is* the time?"

I looked at my watch, and found it was half-past three.

"I thought as much," he muttered. "I'll wring that blessed bird's neck if I get hold of it." And he prepared to go.

"If you can wait half a minute," I said, getting out of bed, "I'll go a bit of the way with you."

"It's very good of you," he rejoined, pausing, "but it seems unkind to drag you out."

"Not at all," I replied; "I shall like a walk." And I partially dressed myself, and took my umbrella; and he put his arm through mine, and we went out together.

Just by the gate we met Jones, one of the local constables. "Good-night, Jones," I said (I always feel affable at Christmas-time).

"Good-night, sir," answered the man a little gruffly, I thought. "May I ask what you're a-doing of ?"

"Oh, it's all right," I responded, with a wave of my umbrella; "I'm just seeing my friend part of the way home." He said, "What friend?"

"Oh, ah, of course," I laughed; "I forgot. He's invisible to you. He is the ghost of the gentleman that killed the wait. I'm just going to the corner with him."

"Ah, I don't think I would, if I was you, sir," said Jones severely. "If you take my advice, you'll say good-bye to your friend here, and go back indoors. Perhaps you are not aware that you are walking about with nothing on but a night-shirt and a pair of boots and an opera-hat. Where's your trousers?"

swearing: saying bad words. **fearfully**: terribly.

absurd: ridiculous. **altogether**: completely.
our old man: our creator.

over and over again: many times.
stick to it: observe it.

handy: convenient.
inquired: asked.
on the point of: about to. **started**: moved suddenly.
distinctly: clearly.

rising: getting up. **reaching**: putting out an arm.
put up with: bear, stand.

I thought as much: I thought so. **muttered**: said in a low tone.
wring: strangle. **blessed**: *substitute for bad word*. **get hold of
it**: find it, catch it.
a bit of: some of.
rejoined: answered.
drag you out: bring you out.
partially: in part.

constables: policemen.
affable: friendly.

gruffly: angrily.
a-doing of: *(dialect)* doing.
wave: movement.
seeing… home: accompanying.

was: *the correct form is "were".*

you are not aware: you do not realize.
Where's: *where are.*

I did not like the man's manner at all. I said, "Jones! I don't wish to have to report you, but it seems to me you've been drinking. My trousers are where a man's trousers ought to be - on his legs. I distinctly remember putting them on."

"Well, you haven't got them on now," he retorted.

"I beg your pardon," I replied. "I tell you I have; I think I ought to know."

"I think so, too," he answered, "but you evidently don't. Now you come along indoors with me, and don't let's have any more of it."

Uncle John came to the door at this point, having been awaked, I suppose, by the altercation; and, at the same moment, Aunt Maria appeared at the window in her nightcap. I explained the constable's mistake to them, treating the matter as lightly as I could, so as not to get the man into trouble, and I turned for confirmation to the ghost.

He was gone! He had left me without a word - without even saying good-bye!

It struck me as so unkind, his having gone off in that way, that I burst into tears; and Uncle John came out, and led me back into the house.

On reaching my room, I discovered that Jones was right. I had not put on my trousers, after all. They were still hanging over the bed-rail. I suppose, in my anxiety not to keep the ghost waiting, I must have forgotten them.

Such are the plain facts of the case, out of which it must, doubtless, to the healthy, charitable mind appear impossible that calumny could spring.

But it has.

Persons - I say "persons"- have professed themselves unable to understand the simple circumstances herein narrated, except in the light of explanations at once misleading and insulting. Slurs have been cast and aspersions made on me by those of my own flesh and blood.

But I bear no ill-feeling. I merely, as I have said, set forth this statement for the purpose of clearing my character from injurious suspicion.

manner: way of speaking.
report you: talk to your superior officer.
ought to: should.

retorted: replied.
I beg your pardon: I'm sorry.

evidently: obviously.

altercation: noisy discussion.
nightcap: cap worn in bed.

constable: policeman.

confirmation: support.

struck: seemed to.
burst into tears: started crying. **led**: took.

discovered: found.

hanging: suspended. **bed-rail**: tube at foot of bed. **anxiety**: agitation.
plain: simple.
doubtless: without any doubt. **healthy**: in good physical condition. **charitable**: kind. **calumny**: lies. **spring**: arise, come out.

professed themselves unable: said they could not. **herein** : in this story.
misleading: giving the wrong impression. **Slurs**: insults. **cast**: thrown. **aspersions**: unpleasant insinuations. **my own flesh and blood**: my own family. **bear**: have, carry. **ill-feeling**: negative sentiments. **merely**: simply. **set forth**: wrote down. **statement**: declaration. **for the purpose**: with the aim. **injurious**: damaging.

A PATHETIC STORY

"Oh! I want you to write the pathetic story for the Christmas number, if you will, old man," said the editor of the — *Weekly Journal* to me, as I poked my head into his den one sunny July morning, some years ago.

"Thomas is anxious to have the comic sketch. He says he overheard a joke last week, that he thinks he can work up. I expect I shall have to do the cheerful love story, about the man that everybody thinks is dead and that turns up on Christmas Eve and marries the girl, myself. I was hoping to get out of it this time, but I'm afraid I can't. Then I shall get Miggs to do the charitable appeal business. I think he's the most experienced man we have now for that; and Skittles can run off the cynical column, about the Christmas bills, and the indigestion: he's always very good in a cynical article, Skittles is; he's got just the correct don't-know-what-he-means-himself sort of touch for it, if you understand."

"Skittles," I may mention, was the nickname we had given to a singularly emotional and seriously inclined member of the staff, whose correct cognomen was Beherhend.

Skittles himself always waxed particularly sentimental over Christmas. During the week preceding that sacred festival, he used to go about literally swelling with geniality and affection for all man and womankind. He would greet comparative strangers with a burst of delight that other men would have found difficult to work up in the case of a rich relation, and would shower upon them the good wishes, always so plentiful and cheap at that season, with such an evident conviction that practical benefit to the wishee would ensue therefrom as to send them away labouring under a vague sense of obligation.

The sight of an old friend at that period was almost dangerous to him. His feelings would quite overcome him. He could not speak. You feared that he would burst.

He was generally quite laid up on Christmas Day itself, owing to having drunk so many sentimental toasts on Christmas Eve. I never saw such a man as Skittles for proposing and drinking sentimental toasts. He would drink to "dear old Christmas-time," and to "dear old England;" and then he would drink to his mother, and all his other

PATHETIC: sad, full of pathos.

number: edition of a newspaper or magazine **old man**: term of affection. **editor**: most important journalist, head of newspaper. **poked**: put. **den**: animal's home, here small office. **anxious**: keen, enthusiastic. **overheard**: heard someone else speaking. **work up**: transform into an article or sketch. **cheerful**: happy. **turns up**: appears. **get out of**: avoid.

charitable appeal: request for money for some charity.

run off: write something easily and quickly. **cynical**: unromantic. **bills**: accounts to pay.

touch: skill, ability. **mention**: say. **nickname**: informal, unofficial name. **singularly**: strangely, unusually. **seriously inclined**: of a serious character. **staff**: group of people working in a particular place. **cognomen**: surname. **waxed**: became. **preceding**: before. **sacred**: holy. **swelling**: expanding. **geniality**: happiness. **womankind**: women. **greet**: say hallo to. **comparative strangers**: people he didn't know very well. **burst**: explosion. **delight**: happiness. **work up**: generate. **shower**: rain. **plentiful**: common, abundant. **cheap**: inexpensive. **season**: time of year. **wishee**: person receiving a good wish. **ensue therefrom**: follow from these good wishes. **labouring**: suffering. **sense of obligation**: feeling that they had to do something to deserve this. **The sight of**: seeing. **quite overcome**: completely take control of. **feared**: worried, were afraid. **burst**: explode. **quite laid up**: very ill, in bed. **owing to**: because of. **toast**: when people drink together and make a dedication.

relations, and to "lovely woman," and "old chums," or he would propose "Friendship," in the abstract, "may it never grow cool in the heart of a true-born Briton," and "Love — may it ever look out at us from the eyes of our sweethearts and wives," or even "The Sun — that is ever shining behind the clouds, dear boys, — where we can't see it, and where it is not of much use to us." He was so full of sentiment, was Skittles! But his favourite toast, and the one over which he would become more eloquently lugubrious than over any other, was always "absent friends". He appeared to be singularly rich in "absent friends". And it must be said for him that he never forgot them. Whenever and wherever liquor was to his hand, Skittles's "absent friends" were sure of a drink, and his present friends, unless they displayed great tact and firmness, of a speech calculated to give them all the blues for a week. Folks did say at one time that Skittles's eyes usually turned in the direction of the county jail when he pledged this toast; but on its being ascertained that Skittles's kindly remembrance was not intended to be exclusive, but embraced everybody else's absent friends as well as his own, the uncharitable suggestion was withdrawn.

Still, we had too much of these "absent friends", however comprehensive a body they may have been. Skittles over-did the business. We all think highly of our friends when they are absent — more highly, as a rule, than we do of them when they are not absent. But we do not want to be always worrying about them. At a Christmas party, or a complimentary dinner to somebody, or at a shareholders' meeting, where you naturally feel good and sad, they are in place, but Skittles dragged them in at the most inappropriate seasons. Never shall I forget his proposing their health once at a wedding. It had been a jolly wedding. Everything had gone off splendidly, and everybody was in the best of spirits. The breakfast was over, and quite all the necessary toasts had been drunk. It was getting near the time for the bride and bridegroom to depart, and we were just thinking about collecting the rice and boots with which to finally bless them, when Skittles rose in his place, with a funereal expression on his countenance and a glass of wine in his hand.

I guessed what was coming in a moment. I tried to kick him under the table. I do not mean, of course, that I tried to kick him there altogether; though I am not at all sure whether,

old chums: old friends.
propose: propose a toast to.
may it never grow cool: I hope it will never die. **true-born Briton**: someone really born in Great Britain. **ever**: always. **sweethearts**: loved ones.

eloquently: expressively. **lugubrious**: unhappy, funereal.
appeared: seemed. **singularly**: unusually.

liquor: alcoholic drink.

unless they displayed: if they did not show. **tact**: diplomacy.
firmness: determination. **speech**: talk. **give them the blues**: make them sad. **Folks**: people.
county jail: local prison. **pledged**: made.
ascertained: discovered, found. **kindly**: friendly.
remembrance: memory.
embraced: included. **uncharitable**: unfriendly.
withdrawn: taken back, retired.

overdid: exaggerated. **highly**: a lot.
as a rule: normally.

complimentary: free.
shareholders' meeting: meeting of the people owning a company. **in place**: suitable. **dragged them in**: used them.
never shall I forget: *Note the inversion.*
proposing their health: drinking to absent friends. **jolly**: happy, enjoyable. **gone off**: happened.
breakfast: wedding meal.

bride and bridegroom: woman and man married.
rice and boots: objects typically used at weddings.
bless: give God's approval to. **rose**: got up. **funereal**: sad.
countenance: face.
guessed: knew. **kick**: hit with the foot.
kick him there altogether: with kicks, send Skittles under the table. **though**: even if. **whether**: if.

under the circumstances, I should not have been justified in going even to that length. What I mean is, that the attempt to kick him took place under the table.

It failed, however. True, I did kick somebody; but it evidently could not have been Skittles, for he remained unmoved. In all probability it was the bride, who was sitting next to him. I did not try again; and he started, uninterfered with, on his favourite theme.

"Friends," he commenced, his voice trembling with emotion, while a tear glistened in his eye, "before we part — some of us, perhaps, never to meet again on earth — before this guileless young couple, who have this day taken upon themselves the manifold trials and troubles of married life, quit the peaceful fold, as it were, to face the bitter griefs and disappointments of this weary life, there is one toast, hitherto undrunk, that I would wish to propose."

Here he wiped away the before-mentioned tear, and the people looked solemn, and endeavoured to crack nuts without making a noise.

"Friends," he went on, growing more and more impressive and dejected in his tones, "there are few of us here who have not at some time or other known what it is to lose, through death or travel, a dear beloved one — maybe two or three."

At this point, he stifled a sob; and the bridegroom's aunt, at the bottom of the table, whose eldest son had lately left the country at the expense of his relations, upon the clear understanding that he would never again return, began to cry quietly into the ice-pudding.

"The fair young maiden at my side," continued Skittles, clearing his throat, and laying his hand tenderly on the bride's shoulder, "as you are all aware, was, a few years ago, bereft of her mother. Ladies and gentlemen, what can be more sad than the death of a mother?"

This, of course, had the effect of starting the bride off sobbing. The bridegroom, meaning well, but, naturally, under the circumstances, nervous and excited, sought to console her by murmuring that he felt sure it had all happened for the best, and that no one who had ever known the old lady would for a moment wish her back again; upon which he was indignantly informed by his newly-made wife that if he was so pleased at her mother's death, it was

to that length: to that extreme. **attempt**: try.

evidently: obvious.
unmoved: in the same place, immobile. **bride**: woman just married.

commenced: began.
glistened: shone, reflected light.

guileless: innocent. **couple**: two people, husband and wife.
manifold: many. **trials and troubles**: difficulties.
quit: leave. **peaceful fold**: peaceful family life. **bitter**: sad and difficult. **griefs**: sadnesses. **disappointments**: things going wrong. **weary**: tired. **hitherto**: until this moment.
wiped away: cleaned.
solemn: serious. **endeavoured**: tried. **crack**: open.

growing: becoming. **impressive**: noble.
dejected: depressed.

stifled: suppressed. **sob**: cry. **bridegroom**: man recently married.
eldest: oldest. **lately**: recently.

understanding: agreement.
ice-pudding: type of dessert.
fair: beautiful. **maiden**: girl.
clearing his throat: making ready to speak.
shoulder: joint between arm and body. **as you are all aware**: as you all know. **bereft of her mother**: lost her mother, her mother died.

sobbing: crying. **meaning well**: with good intentions.
sought: tried.
console: make happy again. **murmuring**: saying in a low voice.
it had all happened for the best: it was generally a positive thing.
wish her back again: wish that the mother returned to life.
indignantly: angrily.
newly-made wife: the woman he had just married.

a pity he had not told her so before, and she would never have married him — and he sank into thoughtful silence. On my looking up, which I had hitherto carefully abstained from doing, my eyes unfortunately encountered those of a brother journalist who was sitting at the other side of the table, and we both burst out laughing, thereupon gaining a reputation for callousness that I do not suppose either of us has outlived to this day.

Skittles, the only human being at that once festive board that did not appear to be wishing he were anywhere else, droned on, with evident satisfaction:

"Friends," he said, "shall that dear mother be forgotten at this joyous gathering? Shall the lost mother, father, brother, sister, child, friend of any of us be forgotten? No, ladies and gentlemen! Let us, amid our merriment, still think of those lost, wandering souls: let us, amid the wine-cup and the blithesome jest, remember — 'Absent Friends'."

The toast was drunk to the accompaniment of suppressed sobs and low moans, and the wedding guests left the table to bathe their faces and calm their thoughts. The bride, rejecting the proffered assistance of the groom, was assisted into the carriage by her father, and departed, evidently full of misgivings as to her chance of future happiness in the society of such a heartless monster as her husband had just shown himself to be!

Skittles has been an "absent friend" himself at that house since then.

But I am not getting on with my pathetic story.

"Do not be late with it," our editor had said. "Let me have it by the end of August, certain. I mean to be early with the Christmas number this time. We didn't get it out till October last year, you know. I don't want the *Clipper* to be before us again!"

"Oh, that will be all right," I had answered, airily. "I shall soon run that off. I've nothing much to do this week. I'll start it at once."

So, as I went home, I cast about in my mind for a pathetic subject to work on. But not a pathetic idea could I think of. Comic fancies crowded in upon me, until my brain began to give way under the strain of holding them; and, if I had not calmed myself down with a last week's *Punch*, I should, in all probability, have gone off in a fit.

sank: fell. **thoughtful**: preoccupied.
hitherto: so far, until now.
abstained from: avoided. **encountered**: met.

burst out laughing: exploded into laughter. **gaining**: getting.
callousness: cruelty.
outlived: lasted longer than.
festive: happy. **board**: table.

droned on: continued in a boring fashion. **evident**: visible.

joyous: full of joy. **gathering**: meeting of people.

amid: in the middle of. **merriment**: celebration.
wandering: moving without direction or aim.
blithesome jest: funny joke.

sobs: crying. **moans**: sounds of misery.
bathe: wash.
rejecting: refusing. **proffered**: offered. **groom**: husband.
evidently: clearly.
misgivings: regrets, worries.
society: company. **heartless**: cruel.

Skittles has been an "absent friend": he has never been invited
to that house again.
getting on: making progress.

mean: intend.
get it out: make it ready for sale.
Clipper: another journal.

airily: lightly.
run that off: write it quickly and easily.
at once: immediately.
cast about: searched, looked for.

Comic: funny. **fancies**: fantasies, ideas.
give way: break down. **strain**: stress.
Punch: English humorous magazine.
fit: convulsion.

"Oh, I'm evidently not in the humour for pathos," I said to myself. "It is no use trying to force it. I've got plenty of time. I will wait till I feel sad."

But as the days went on, I merely grew more and more cheerful. By the middle of August, matters were becoming serious. If I could not, by some means or other, contrive to get myself into a state of the blues during the next week or ten days, there would be nothing in the Christmas number of the — *Weekly Journal* to make the British public wretched, and its reputation as a high-class paper for the family circle would be irretrievably ruined!

I was a conscientious young man in those days. I had undertaken to write a four-and-a-half column pathetic story by the end of August; and if — no matter at what mental or physical cost to myself — the task could be accomplished, those four columns and a half should be ready.

I have generally found indigestion a good breeder of sorrowful thoughts. Accordingly, for a couple of days I lived upon an exclusive diet of hot boiled pork, Yorkshire pudding, and assorted pastry, with lobster salad for supper. It gave me comic nightmares. I dreamed of elephants trying to climb trees, and of churchwardens being caught playing pitch-and-toss on Sundays, and woke up shaking with laughter! I abandoned the dyspeptic scheme, and took to reading all the pathetic literature I could collect together. But it was of no use. The little girl in Wordsworth's "We are Seven" only irritated me; wanted to slap her. Byron's blighted pirates bored me. When, in a novel, the heroine died, I was glad; and when the author told me that the hero never smiled again on earth, I did not believe it.

As a last resource, I re-perused one or two of my own concoctions. They made me feel ashamed of myself, but not exactly miserable — at least, not miserable in the way I wanted to be miserable.

Then I bought all the standard works of wit and humour that had ever been published, and waded steadily through the lot. They lowered me a good deal, but not sufficiently. My cheerfulness seemed proof against everything.

One Saturday evening I went out and hired a man to come in and sing sentimental ballads to me. He earned his money (five shillings). He sang me everything dismal there was in English, Scotch, Irish, and Welsh, together with a few

humour: mood.
plenty of: lots of, more than enough.

merely: only, simply. **grew**: became.
cheerful: happy. **matters**: things.
by some means or other: in any way. **contrive**: manage,
succeed. **state of the blues**: sadness.

wretched: miserable, unhappy.
irretrievably: completely, without hope of recovery. **ruined**:
destroyed. **conscientious**: hard working and serious.
undertaken: promised.

task: work. **accomplished**: done, finished.

breeder: generator, producer.
sorrowful: very sad. **Accordingly**: so.
Yorkshire pudding: typical English dish made with flour and
milk; used to accompany meat dishes. **assorted**: various. **pastry**:
pies and cakes. **nightmares**: bad dreams. **climb**: go up.
 churchwardens: minor church officials. **pitch-and-toss**: low
class game.
abandoned: left. **dyspeptic**: bad digestion.

slap: hit. **blighted**: unlucky.
heroine: female protagonist.
glad: happy.

resource: possibility. **re-perused**: looked at again.
concoctions: works. **ashamed**: embarrassed.

standard: most common. **wit**: clever words.
waded: crossed a river on foot.
waded steadily through the lot: read them all slowly. **lowered**:
depressed. **a good deal**: a lot. **cheerfulness**: happiness. **proof**:
safe. **hired**: paid money for services.
ballads: songs. **earned his money**: performed a good service.
dismal: depressing.

translations from the German; and, after the first hour and a half, I found myself unconsciously trying to dance to the different tunes. I invented some really pretty steps for "Auld Robin Grey," winding up with a quaint flourish of the left leg at the end of each verse.

At the beginning of the last week, I went to my editor and laid the case before him.

"Why, what's the matter with you?" he said. "You used to be so good at that sort of thing! Have you thought of the poor girl who loves the young man that goes away and never comes back, and she waits and waits, and never marries, and nobody knows that her heart is breaking?"

"Of course I have!" I retorted, rather irritably. "Do you think I don't know the rudiments of my profession?"

"Well," he remarked, "won't it do?"

"No," I answered. "With marriage such a failure as it seems to be all round now-a-days, how can you pump up sorrow for anyone lucky enough to keep out of it?"

"Um," he mused, "how about the child that tells everybody not to cry, and then dies?"

"Oh, and a good riddance to it!" I replied, peevishly. "There are too many children in this world. Look what a noise they make, and what a lot of money they cost in boots!"

My editor agreed that I did not appear to be in the proper spirit to write a pathetic child-story.

He inquired if I had thought of the old man who wept over the faded love-letters on Christmas Eve; and I said that I had, and that I considered him an old idiot.

"Would a dog story do?" he continued: "something about a dead dog; that's always popular."

"Not Christmassy enough," I argued.

The betrayed maiden was suggested; but dismissed, on reflection, as being too broad a subject for the pages of a "Companion for the Home Circle"—our sub-title.

"Well, think it over for another day," said my editor. "I don't want to have to go to Jenks. He can only be pathetic as a costermonger, and our lady readers don't always like the expressions."

I thought I would go and ask the advice of a friend of mine — a very famous and popular author; in fact, one of the *most* famous and popular authors of the day. I was very proud of his friendship, because he was a very great man indeed: not great,

unconsciously: without realizing it.
tunes: melodies. **steps**: dance movements.
"Auld Robin Grey": Scottish tune. **winding up**: finishing. **quaint**: strange. **flourish**: decorative movement.

laid the case before him: explained everything to him.

retorted: answered.
rudiments: fundamentals, basic principles.
won't it do: isn't it good enough.

all round: everywhere. **pump up**: generate.
sorrow: sadness. **keep out of it**: not get married.
mused: meditated.

good riddance to it: we're better without it. **peevishly**: irritably.

inquired: asked. **wept**: cried.
faded: old and indistinct.

do: be alright, serve the purpose.

argued: reasoned.
betrayed: deceived, tricked. **maiden**: girl. **dismissed**: rejected, refused. **on reflection**: after thinking. **broad**: wide.

costermonger: worker from the markets, vulgar in nature.

author: writer.

perhaps, in the earnest meaning of the word; not great like the greatest men — the men who do not know that they are great — but decidedly great, according to the practical standard. When he wrote a book, a hundred thousand copies would be sold during the first week; and when a play of his was produced, the theatre was crammed for five hundred nights. And of each new work it was said that it was more clever and grand and glorious than were even the works he had written before.

Wherever the English language was spoken, his name was an honoured household word. Wherever he went, he was fêted and lionized and cheered. Descriptions of his charming house, of his charming sayings and doings, of his charming self, were in every newspaper.

Shakespeare was not one-half so famous in his day as — is in his.

Fortunately, he happened to be still in town; and on being ushered into his sumptuously-furnished study, I found him sitting before one of the windows, smoking an after-dinner cigar.

He offered me one from the same box. — 's cigars are not to be refused. I know he pays half-a-crown a-piece for them by the hundred; so I accepted, lit up, and, sitting down opposite to him, told him my trouble.

He did not answer immediately after I had finished; and I was just beginning to think that he could not have been listening, when — with his eyes looking out through the open window to where, beyond the smoky city, it seemed as if the sun, in passing through, had left the gates of the sky ajar behind him — he took his cigar from his lips, and said: "Do you want a real pathetic story? I can tell you one if you do. It is not very long, but it is sad enough."

He spoke in so serious a tone that almost any reply seemed out of place and I remained silent.

"It is the story of a man who lost his own self," he continued, still looking out upon the dying light, as though he read the story there, "who stood by the death-bed of himself, and saw himself slowly die, and knew that he was dead — for ever.

"Once upon a time there lived a poor boy. He had little in common with other children. He loved to wander by himself, to think and dream all day. It was not that he was morose, or did not care for his comrades, only that something within kept whispering to his childish heart that he had

earnest: serious.

decidedly: definitely. **according to**: following.

crammed: crowded with people.

household word: known everywhere.
fêted: celebrated. **lionized**: made into a hero. **cheered**: applauded. **charming**: pretty, in good taste.

Fortunately: luckily.
ushered into: shown into, accompanied by servants. **sumptuously**: richly. **before**: in front of.

half-a-crown: two shillings and sixpence. **a-piece**: each.
by the hundred: in orders of a hundred. **lit up**: lit the cigar.
trouble: problem.

smoky: grey.
gates: doors.
ajar: not completely closed.

wander: walk without any particular direction.

morose: miserable. **care for**: like. **comrades**: friends.
within: inside him. **kept**: continued. **whispering**: speaking very softly.

deeper lessons to comprehend than his schoolmates had. And an unseen hand would lead him away into the solitude where alone he could learn their meaning.

"Ever amid the babel of the swarming street, would he hear strong, silent voices, speaking to him as he walked, telling him of the work that would one day be entrusted to his hands, — work for God, such as is given to only the very few to do, work for the helping of God's children in the world, for the making of them stronger and truer and higher; — and, in some dimly-lighted corner, where for a moment they were alone, he would stand and raise his boyish hands to Heaven, and thank God for this great promised gift of noble usefulness, and pray that he might ever prove worthy of the trust; and, in the joy of his coming work, the little frets of life floated like drift-wood on a deepening river; and as he grew, the voices spoke to him ever more plainly, until he saw his work before him clearly, as a traveller on the hill-top sees the pathway through the vale.

"And so the years passed, and he became a man, and his labour lay ready to his hand.

"And then a foul demon came and tempted him — the demon that has killed many a better man before, that will kill many a great man yet — the demon of worldly success. And the demon whispered evil words into his ear, and, God forgive him! — he listened.

" 'Of what good to *you*, think you, will it be, your writing mighty truths and noble thoughts? What will the world pay for *them*? What has ever been the reward of the earth's greatest teachers and poets — the men who have given their lives to the best service of mankind — but neglect and scorn and poverty? Look around! what are the wages of the few earnest workers of today but a pauper's pittance, compared with the wealth that is showered down on those who jig to the tune that the crowd shouts for? Aye, the true singers are honoured when they are dead — those that are remembered; and the thoughts from their brains once fallen, whether they themselves are remembered or not, stir, with ever-widening circles to all time, the waters of human life. But of what use is that to themselves, who starved? You have talent, genius. Riches, luxury, power can be yours — soft beds and dainty foods. You can be great in the greatness that the world can see, famous with fame your own ears will hear. Work for the

deeper: more serious. **comprehend**: understand. **schoolma-tes**: school companions. **unseen**: invisible. **lead him away**: take him. **solitude**: loneliness.
amid: in the middle of. **babel**: madness, confusion. **swarming**: full of busy people.
entrusted: given.

dimly-lighted: badly illuminated.
raise: lift up.

ever: always. **prove worthy of the trust**: be good enough to justify God's confidence in him. **frets**: worries. **drift-wood**: wood carried by the water. **deepening**: becoming deeper.
plainly: clearly.
hill-top: summit of a hill. **pathway**: road for walking on. **vale**: valley.
labour: work.
foul: horrible, evil. **tempted**: led into temptation.

worldly: material, temporal.
whispered: said very quietly.
forgive: pardon.

mighty: strong.
reward: prize, thanks.

but: except. **neglect**: lack of attention.
scorn: negative attitude. **poverty**: being poor. **wages**: weekly pay. **earnest**: serious. **pauper**: person without any money at all. **pittance**: extremely small amount of money. **wealth**: riches.
that is showered down on: that rains on, that comes down on.
jig: dance. **tune**: melody. **Aye**: yes.

stir: move. **ever-widening**: becoming wider and wider.

starved: died of hunger. **luxury**: beautiful and expensive things.
dainty: delicate.

world, and the world will pay you promptly; the wages the gods give are long delayed.'

"And the demon prevailed over him, and he fell.

"And, instead of being the servant of God, he became the slave of men. And he wrote for the multitude what they wanted to hear, and the multitude applauded and flung money to him, and as he would stoop to pick it up, he would grin and touch his cap, and tell them how generous and noble they were.

"And the spirit of the artist that is handmaiden to the spirit of the prophet departed from him, and he grew into the clever huckster, the smart tradesman, whose only desire was to discover the public taste that he might pander to it.

" 'Only tell me what it is you like,' he would cry in his heart, 'that I may write it for you, good people! Will you have again the old lies? Do you still love the old dead conventions, the worn-out formulas of life, the rotting weeds of evil thoughts that keep the fresh air from the flowers?

" 'Shall I sing again to you the childish twaddle you have heard a million times before? Shall I defend for you the wrong, and call it right? Shall I stab Truth in the back for you, or praise it?

" 'How shall I flatter you today, and in what way tomorrow and the next day? Only tell me what you wish me to say, what you wish me to think, that I may say it and think it, good people, and so get your pence and your plaudits!'

"Thus he became rich and famous and great; and had fine clothes to wear and rich foods to eat, as the demon had promised him, and servants to wait on him, and horses, and carriages to ride in; and he would have been happy — as happy as such things can make a man — only that at the bottom of his desk there lay (and he had never had the courage to destroy them) a little pile of faded manuscripts, written in boyish hand, that would speak to him of the memory of a poor lad who had once paced the city's feet-worn stones, dreaming of no other greatness than that of being one of God's messengers to men, and who had died, and had been buried for all eternity, long years ago."

It was a very sad story, but not exactly the sort of sad story, I felt, that the public wants in a Christmas number. So I had to fall back upon the broken-hearted maiden, after all!

promptly: quickly. **wages**: pay.
delayed: late.
prevailed: was stronger.   **fell**: gave in to temptation.

multitude: masses.
applauded: shouted their approval. **flung**: threw.
stoop: move down.
grin: smile.

handmaiden: servant.
prophet: person predicting things. **departed from**: left.
huckster: charlatan.   **smart**: clever, cunning.   **tradesman**: commercial dealer. **pander to it**: satisfy it.

lies: things which are not true.
worn-out: exhausted, without meaning. **rotting**: decaying, not fresh. **weeds**: parasitic plants. **evil**: bad.
twaddle: nonsense.
stab: cut with a sword or knife.
praise: say good things about.
flatter: tell someone good things about himself.

plaudits: approval.

wait on him: serve him.

faded: old and indistinct. **manuscripts**: documents written by hand. **boyish**: childish.
lad: boy. **paced**: walked.
feet-worn stones: the stones consumed by many people walking over them.

number: edition of a newspaper or magazine.
fall back upon: make use of as a last resort. **maiden**: girl.

Comprehension Questions

– A Personal Explanation –

1. In what way is this story different from the others?
2. Why is this not "a story"?
3. What is the main reason he is so reluctant to tell this story?
4. What does he say modern writers have a strong objection to doing?
5. What adjectives does he use to describe his story?
6. What are the reasons which make him tell his story?

– My own Story –

1. Where does he decide to spend the night?
2. What are his uncle's objections to his proposal?
3. Why does he think the spirits will not harm him?
4. Why do you think he sits on Mr Coombes and mistakes Biffles for his uncle?
5. What is his priviledge as "the guest"?
6. How does he go upstairs? What does he feel like doing?
7. What does the candle keep doing?
8. What does he eventually do with the candle?
9. What does he do while lying in bed?
10. When does he first notice the ghost?
11. Why is it strange that the ghost looks happy?
12. What does he first think on seeing the ghost?
13. How does he know it's a ghost?
14. Why is he pleased to see the ghost?
15. Why is he "somewhat staggered" at the ghost's answer to his question about the wait?
16. How does the ghost react at the suggestion he only "had a hand" in the death of the organ-grinder?
17. How many cornet-players has he killed?
18. What is meant by "he thought there were few ghosts who could look back upon a life of more sustained usefulness"?
19. How does he get rid of the "young lady who was learning to play the guitar" and the gentleman who practiced on the bass-viol?
20. What happens to the couple?
21. What does he do to muffin-men?
22. Who else and in what manner does he kill?
23. Why does the ghost doubt whether he will come next Christmas Eve?
24. What does a cock crow mean to ghosts? Why does the ghost think this is unfair?
25. Why does the writer dress in such a hurry?
26. Why does the contable stop him?
27. What is the the reason for the "slurs and aspersions"?

78

– A Pathetic Story –

1. What does the editor want him to do?
2. Why is it strange that the editor thinks Skittles is the right man to do the "cynical column"?
3. How does Skittles behave before Christmas?
4. What is meant by "he would shower upon them good wishes, … as to send them away labouring under a vague sense of obligation"?
5. What happens when Skittles sees an old friend in that period?
6. Why is Skittles "generally quite laid up on Christmas Day itself"?
7. What is Skittles's favourite toast?
8. Why do Skittles's toasts to "absent friends" cause his present friends to suffer "the blues for a week"?
9. What is suggested by "Skittles's eyes usually turned in the direction of the county jail when he pledged the toast"?
10. Why is the "uncharitable suggestion" withdrawn?
11. What is meant by "We all think highly of our friends when they are absent - more highly, as a rule, than we do of them when they are not absent"?
12. Why does the writer say Skittles "overdid the business"?
13. On what occasions are Skittles's toasts to "absent friends" suitable?
14. How do the people at the wedding feel before Skittles proposes his toast?
15. What does the writer do in an effort to stop him?
16. Who are particularly affected by his toast at the wedding?
17. How does the bridegroom try to console his wife? What is the result?
18. Why do you think the writer and his "brother journalist" burst out laughing? What does this do to their reputations?
19. Do you think it is strange that Skittles "has been 'an absent friend' at that house since then"? Why? Why not?
20. Why does the writer find it difficult to write his "pathetic story"?
21. What methods does he use to get "into a state of the blues"? What are the results?
22. What stories does the editor suggest? Why are they rejected?
23. Why is he proud of his friendship with the famous author?
24. Tell in your own words the author's pathetic story?
25. Who is the story about?
26. Why doesn't the writer use the story? What does he write about?

CONTENTS

Jerome Klapka Jerome (1859 - 1927) was born in Walsall, England. He is famous for his elegant humour and lively comedy. His most famous books *("Three men on a boat" , "Three men on the Bummel")*, written in the last decade of the nineteenth century, combine lively observation of the social ironies of Victorian England with a comic and sentimental vein which make them irresistible to a wide audience. He achieved great popularity with these books, which were translated into many languages. He also produced some brilliant journalism, in particular between 1892 and 1897. He died in Northampton, England.